Hygge

the Art *of* Minimalism

2 IN 1 BUNDLE

OLIVIA TELFORD

HYGGE AND THE ART OF MINIMALISM: 2 in 1 Bundle
by Olivia Telford

ISBN-10: 1670831590
ISBN-13: 978-1670831590

HYGGE

*DISCOVERING THE DANISH ART OF HAPPINESS —
HOW TO LIVE COZILY AND ENJOY
LIFE'S SIMPLE PLEASURES*

OLIVIA TELFORD

CONTENTS

INTRODUCTION

Hygge (pronounced "HOO-ga") is a Danish and Scandinavian concept that describes a personal feeling rather than an abstract concept. In other words, the experience of Hygge is felt within an individual's body and is not just something merely understood by the mind. The boiled-down meaning is "coziness," but the high-level meaning is an approach to living. Hygge embraces the idea of positivity and enjoyment that comes from everyday experiences. Cultivating this type of mindset requires an individual to pay better attention to their mind and surroundings. This idea permeates the core concepts and overall attitudes about life and how people Denmark, and the wider Nordic region, live. This book will focus predominantly on the ways that Danes experience hygge and how other Westerners can also experience it.

Hygge is not merely a noun, but it is also a verb and an adjective. It is a diversified term used to describe a scenario, emotion, and way of life that centers itself on the idea of "being cozy." While this is quite a broad definition, it allows the person who implements it the freedom to decide what it means for them, which is cozy in and of itself. The additional benefit is that the concept is fluid and moldable to anyone's circumstances and preferences because an individual experiences hygge uniquely. In other words, no matter who you are, you can implement and benefit from hygge.

Therefore, anything you decide is cozy and comfortable could be considered hygge. Whether that is soft lighting, a roaring fire, walking around your home naked, cuddling with a loved one, or even the repetitive movements of shaving. If it is something comforting, you can define it as hygge. It also extends outside of the home. It can be walks in nature, feeding ducks at a lake, or going out to eat at your favorite restaurant. Whatever you decide to be hygge is hygge for you. It's not a one-size-fits-all concept, but it is a concept that fits all sizes! Confusing, right? No worries! This book will clear that up.

But if you look at hygge from this particular angle, you'd think it was just an adjective, right? Well, something merely described as comfortable is simply that. However, the word "hygge" is also a noun, and it is derived from the symbolic interpretation placed on an inanimate object or a living person. For instance, if someone walks into an antique shop and finds the atmosphere calming and feels joyful and at peace, that antique shop is hygge for them. That shop is a physical manifestation of an inner feeling they experience when stepping through its doors. In that way, "hygge" is a noun. Certain jewelry, like a ring, could be considered hygge; as could a favorite t-shirt.

However, as stated above, Hygge is also a verb. And in the Danish lifestyle, hygge is a way of life. People who desire Hygge in Denmark actively strive for it every day. In the same way that many Americans strive to stuff in everything they can into each day before they close their eyes at night, Danes focus on hygge to be their lifestyle. Not only is hygge strived for, but other people praise it. In this way, it comprises a positive feedback loop, both internal and external, keeping hygge as a focus even more straightforward.

It sounds like a dream, doesn't it?

So, it is essential to remember that hygge means different things to different people. Throughout this book, you will learn various ways to implement hygge into your life, but it will always be up to you to decide precisely what it means to you. Think of this book as an exploratory guide and not as a set of instructions. Your reading and implementation of concepts in this book should be fun and not a chore, so be sure to bring flexibility and creativity when you implement hygge into your life. Hey, even while I was writing this book, I experienced hygge myself!

Helen Russell, an author and active member of her Danish community, defines hygge as a total absence of things that might annoy you, stress you out, or cause you to become emotionally overwhelmed. She also points out that hygge requires prioritizing people in your life whom you love and feel at ease around.

In other words, her definition is surrounding yourself with things and people that take your stress away and make you feel comfortable. Again, this can mean different things to different people. It also determines everything from what you eat for breakfast, to how you decorate your house, to what scent you decide to put in your car. It means you can decide whether small family gatherings, large gatherings of friends and family, or mostly solitude is hygge-like to you. The best thing with this approach is that you can use hygge to fit your needs or overhaul your personality to fit your new hygge lifestyle. Cool, right?

Americans, English-speaking Canadians, and many other native English speakers have trouble understanding the word "hygge" because it is impossible to translate precisely and accurately. There is no word other than "cozy" to capture the feeling, though many Danes will be quick to tell you that the word cozy lacks the essence of living hygge. The best description I've heard from a Dane translating it to English is:

"the enraptured enjoyment of the simple things in life," but even this characterization is lacking. Language has its limitations on expressing individual emotional states, and for hygge, it is no different. However, sometimes using language to highlight an image can be beneficial. Remember those commercials where a family was gathered in front of a fire, sitting around a dinner table packed with their favorite foods, or gathered on the couch enjoying their favorite movie, and the words "ENJOY THE FINER THINGS IN LIFE" would scroll across the screen? Well, that is an excellent foundation to build on when you begin your journey into the hygge lifestyle. You should make sure to enjoy the finer things in life, but not so much that you overindulge. Suppose you find comfort in eating chocolate cake, great! But if you eat a whole cake every day, you're unlikely to feel comfortable in your body due to the adverse effects of eating unhealthily. Hygge is about balance in your life, so pay attention to this balance as much as possible.

It is understandably frustrating to many that hygge does not have a direct translation. But hey—some of the best things this world has to offer defy precise definition. Have you ever heard someone say, "I couldn't even begin to describe how I felt"? Well, that's similar to hygge. Despite what the term lacks in verbal definition, it makes up for in physical and emotional experiences that produce positive reactions in the body. Even though language is an excellent way to frame experience, it is not always sophisticated enough to define various concepts accurately.

Hygge is such an essential part of the Danish culture and is so innate that they integrate it into their lifestyle with minimal effort. Those 15-minute hot cocoa sessions they give themselves to wind down their day are a defining feature of how they live their life. The relaxation and stress-free environment small rituals like this provide Danes is similar to a quick cup of coffee in a disposable cup is for Americans. These little moments of comfort help brighten up even the darkest of days, making hygge an indispensable tool to facilitate overall well-being.

One reason why I think it's so important to learn from hygge is that Denmark consistently tops the Forbes chart of The World's 10 Happiest Countries. Year after year, it remains within the top three, and many of those years, it inhabits the #1 spot. This success is no fluke, and many Danes proclaim it is the hygge lifestyle that keeps everyone happier. It permeates every aspect of society—rich or poor, male or female, young or old. It is because hygge is so far-reaching and applicable that collectively, regardless of background, the country's population remains happier than most others nearly all of the time.

One of the best parts of living a hygge lifestyle is that it doesn't require a substantial bank account. This lifestyle exists within the confines of what an individual sees as satisfying, stress-relieving, and happiness-inducing. For some, a special scent wafting from the melted wax of a vanilla candle is enough to release enough serotonin to induce what we, as humans, experience as "happiness" and "relaxation." A short jog around the neighborhood might satisfy another person. A few minutes to breathe deeply can induce hygge. Whatever brings you more happiness in your life is likely to help you in your quest to foster a hygge-mindset. And let's face it, many people in this small world of ours could use a little more happiness in their lives.

The principle behind the hygge philosophy sprouts from the seed of 'not doing too much.' Simply put, happiness and stress-relieving environments only exist within small intervals of our existence because we often cram too many activities into our days. Our incessant busy-ness is a self-inflicted poison, but that allows the self-inducement of the hygge-flavored antidote. With a hygge mindset, we can learn to free up more time to give ourselves more comfort. Better yet, we can liberate ourselves from the mentality that work comes before everything else and learn to focus on other things in life that truly matter to us.

Within the hygge lifestyle, you will discover moments of 'hyggelig;' meaning that a specific moment is full of hygge. These moments bring about calm, emotionally stable, and relaxing moods. Perhaps when you sink into a warm bath, you can define the moment as hyggelig. Maybe it's the first time you sit on the sofa after a busy day. When you experience these moments, remember to think of them as hyggelig. Using this type of language will help you cultivate the hygge mindset, which will allow you to draw greater comfort from your day-to-day life, improving your overall well-being.

For many Danes, if you ask them to define "hygge," they won't know what to say. It is like asking Americans to define "optimistic" and why they think it's essential to have energy and enthusiasm for going to work. The idea and concept are so ingrained in the American culture that it permeates our television shows and even our own lives. If someone asked an American to define "optimistic," they might start explaining that it means you act positively at all times. Better yet, ask them why they tend to be so enthusiastic, and they are likely unable to define why. American culture teaches you that you can be or do anything if you put your mind to it. While this is brilliant in some respects as Americans tend to have greater self-confidence than those of other nationalities, it can also be detrimental when Americans over-inflate their abilities through optimism and at the expense of a more nuanced sense of reality.

For Danes, defining "hygge" comes with a similar reaction of uncertainty. In trying to do so, they will likely pause, contemplate, and then try to find the right word or sentence to describe something ingrained in the fibers of their being and beyond adequate description. They might have a "go-to" way of describing what it is, but they will always find it inadequate.

Despite this, Danes do a fantastic job of living the lifestyle and that's the essential part of hygge. Why spend time trying to define something when you could use that time trying to live something? The latter is far more rewarding.

For many Danes, hygge is a form of intimacy. A hygge follower's goal is to create an intentional, intimate surrounding that induces specific chemical reactions within the brain that promote stress relief, contentment, and relaxation. And, as they will make sure to let you know, a follower will induce these reactions purposefully. Creating these atmospheres is paramount for them and is as second nature as going to the bathroom. Some slip in and out of these moments of hygge, but many live this lifestyle throughout their day. Again, it depends on the individual how much hygge they want to fit into every day.

So, instead of continuing to define "hygge," let's take a look at the health benefits that come with living this sort of lifestyle—because there are many that will benefit your life to no end.

It is common knowledge that deep, intentional relaxation and meditation have been known to help with anxiety disorders and depression. It is also common knowledge that stress, left unchecked by personal regulation or a doctor, can lead to sleeping problems, lack of focus and mental acuity, social withdrawal, and many other issues. These issues can compound each other, meaning sleeping problems can worsen anxiety and depression adversely over time, and vice-versa.

However, did you know that the most common ways doctors tell people to relieve their stress are all things found within the hygge lifestyle?

Well, now you do! The top three most recommended methods to use if you are struggling with your stress levels or depression are socializing with people you love and enjoy the company of, getting regular physical activity, and implementing frequent relaxation techniques (such as meditation, deep breathing, or getting a massage). These activities remind an individual that it is within their power to heal themselves and prevent further negativity in their lives.

All of these methods and thousands more fall under the category of living a hygge lifestyle. Is it any wonder that Denmark is so high up on those world happiness charts? Most Americans have to be told by doctors, counselors, and therapists to implement various lifestyle, dietary changes, and techniques to improve their mood. On the other hand, Danes naturally work these techniques into their everyday lives. Once you learn to make positive habits second nature, your life will improve drastically—so make hygge living a positive habit that you seek out as much as possible!

Living a hygge lifestyle encompasses elements of many "cop-out" slogans and platitudes we tend to hear often. It takes a little "don't be so hard on yourself" and wraps it up in a "live a little" blanket before tucking it into bed alongside a healthy dose of "just kick up your feet and relax." These somewhat foreign ideas to the average American of "slow down" and "take it easy" and "do something you enjoy" are all common threads that allow Danish people to be happy and satisfied people. Perhaps you can take comfort that the Western world does pay attention to these concepts sometimes. Look no further than the British poster shown just before World War II that encouraged citizens to "keep calm and carry on" as an example. This attitude is ingrained in Britons, and you can see it everywhere, from mugs to the sides of buses to posters in people's homes.

Danes who follow the hygge lifestyle are not trying to convince you that their lives are somehow perfect. There are plenty of Danes who do not enjoy their jobs, fight with their spouses, or have stress raising their children. What is different about their culture is that they do not accept this feeling of anxiety, worry, and uptightness as an unavoidable part of their everyday lives. They engage in purposeful activities and habits to actively abolish it. They make it a point to "enjoy the finer things in life." They enjoy things that we often dismiss as lazy or self-indulgent. But things like lying down for twenty minutes if it's needed command status within Scandinavian cultures. Because of that, Danes lead happier lives than over 60% of the world's population. The difference then is that when many Americans put their feet up, they feel guilty about not working hard enough. But these moments are fundamental to life's enjoyment, and they should be utilized with balance—no more feeling bad for relaxing. Your body, mind, and soul all need it!

There has to be a way that Danes find happiness within their lives that they swear are just "everyday lives." Because Danish lives can still be full of stress and worry—one moment someone is trying to cook and their child is dumping flour on the floor, another moment a boss comes down on someone else with hard deadlines, and parents expect their offspring to travel long distances for the holidays. So, even by the Western world's definitions, Danish lives are typical in this respect. We can expect to experience similar things.

Yet Danes are happy. Why?

The answer lies within the insight, implementation, and lifestyle of hygge. When you read this book, you will gain and cultivate all these by incorporating hygge into your life.

In this book, you will learn how to implement those moments of hygge and comfort more regularly into your day-to-day. Hygge is not here to change your life; it is here to enhance it. If you're ready for some Danish-style means of self-improvement, you're in the right place.

Welcome, reader, to the reassuring and comforting world of the hygge lifestyle. It is ready for you as soon as you are ready.

JOIN OUR HYGGE GROUP

To maximize the value you receive from this book, join our tight-knit community on Facebook. Here, we focus on sharing experiences to gain more prosperity, abundance, and happiness. It is a safe place to connect and share with other like-minded readers to continue your growth.

It would be great to connect with you there.

Stay well,

Olivia Telford

To Join, Visit:
www.pristinepublish.com/hyggegroup

DOWNLOAD THE AUDIO VERSION OF THIS BOOK FREE

If you love listening to audiobooks on-the-go or enjoy narration as you read along, I have great news for you. You can download the audio book version of *Hygge and The Art of Minimalism: 2 in 1 Bundle* for FREE (Regularly $19.95) just by signing up for a FREE 30-day audible trial!

Visit: www.pristinepublish.com/audiobooks

CHAPTER 1:

WHERE DOES HYGGE COME FROM?

In a technical sense, the word "hygge" derives itself from a Norwegian word meaning "well-being." It first appeared in Danish writings in the 19th-century and has since evolved to encompass an entire cultural phenomenon known most prominently in Denmark. But this definition is just the technical aspect of its linguistic history, though, and every Dane you will ever come across will likely think of every other word in their language before deeming hygge "technical." As we explored in the introduction, hygge is an emotional term. It has no specific meaning, but it can encompass all aspects of an individual's life. Its definition isn't apparent in that respect, so let's explore the history of the term and its application.

You may be less interested in where the term "hygge" comes from and more interested in its evolution. For us to consider this, there are a variety of questions we need to ask. How did hygge evolve into what it means today? How do we implement it in our own lives? Does hygge have a specific color, slogan, or mascot? Does it have an enthusiastic following? Does it have a book of directions or a user guide? Does it have rules, regulations, or expectations? How did it come to be in practice?

In Denmark, there are many different factors as to why hygge took off. First of all, their climate is mostly dark and cold, with winter being the longest season of the year, which means that the Danes spend a great deal of time bundled up indoors. So, their lifestyle of hygge has evolved to implement things they can enjoy inside. The limitation of having to be inside has led Danes to be more creative with their living spaces to make them as comfortable as possible, inducing a hygge state of mind. Inside a Danish house you often find what we see in stereotypical pictures: warm socks, soft candles, a roaring fireplace, and a comfortable blanket slung over the knees. But that is merely one person's version of hygge. Other Danes set up their houses somewhat differently, and they also might feel hygge in other moments that have nothing to do with winter at all.

Even though we may think of Denmark as a country full of remote cabins in the wilderness, hygge does not necessarily mean isolation. For Danes who are cooped up during their harsher winter months, life is usually bustling with friends and family. Some evenings Danes bring families and loved ones together. They consume hot food and cold wine over good conversation, share laughter among old friends, and punctuate these experiences with the scent of smoke caused by a roaring log fire flicking its orange and red fingers towards the chimney. Hygge, in this context, is an intimate setting of togetherness that releases stress, frees the mind, and helps folks unwind from the pressures of life. In this context, hygge is social and full of love. The outside may be cold, but the house is full of warmth.

In this particular instance, then, your hygge is more personal rather than directional. In other words, what it invokes in the individual determines whether it is hygge or not.

Hygge is felt in the very being of the person implementing the hygge lifestyle. In American culture, a "lifestyle" often comes with rules and limitations, like a strict diet or a new exercise program. There is a "1-2-3" and a "step-by-step" to the dance of something new. There is a constraining discipline as well as uncertainty. However, a lot of these rules get broken almost before a person begins. If you try to put too many limitations on your life, a part of you will want to rebel, and a strict diet can lead to a binge that may never have happened before the diet was implemented. Because hygge does not have specific rules or instructions, it can be frustrating to understand precisely what it means to you at first. But have no fear, as over time it will become clearer and more apparent as to what hygge means to you.

Remember that the individual is an essential factor in determining hygge because, remember, hygge is felt, not defined.

What Americans may be missing is the conscious part of their awareness in developing hygge in their lives. Once they work out this problem, the implementation of hygge may become second nature. In Denmark, hygge and the idea of carving out times of hygge started as a more conscious pursuit and has taken place throughout their lifetime. It is, therefore, easier for them to implement it naturally. One of the goals of hygge could be to implement it so often that you no longer have to think about it. Hygge may eventually become as simple to you as taking a breath.

Many Americans tend to bring work home with them and respond to the pressure that they think they need to be "always-on" at all hours of the day. However, a Dane will likely spend less time bringing work home and more time with hygge-like family and friend engagements. The reason Danes find it challenging to define and describe its origins to us is because the effort they put into hygge is natural and would likely have been passed down to them culturally since they were born. Just like people make a conscious effort to drive by a coffee shop to grab a steaming cup of latte macchiato, Danes make a conscious effort to carve out slow and intimate moments with people they treasure. If you ask someone to give up their morning coffee run in the US, they might look at you with a dumbfounded expression and laugh off your suggestion. A Dane would react similarly to that suggestion if you asked them to give up their hygge. It is at least a habit that serves them well, and at most a fundamental part of their DNA!

Many people also look at Denmark and see other factors that could contribute to their life satisfaction: they have universal healthcare, free college education, and shorter workdays. Is hygge, then, a way to profit off others and peddle some sort of "item" to purchase? Not exactly. Danes tend to look at the overly stressful consumerist systems—prevalent especially in the US—and wonder why people are not implementing hygge into their lives, which they believe is nothing more than common sense. To Danes, the way Americans run their lives, operate their educational system, construct their workdays, and dole out their healthcare is nothing short of crazy. They chuckle when Americans discuss their ideas about being "progressive" because the same practices are practically ancient for the Danish.

What is essential to understand about the stereotypical perception of hygge is that the pictures we see that are deemed "hygge" are merely manifestations of how hygge is interpreted and represented within one distinct culture. Because the Danish spend a great deal of time in the dark and inside their homes, they always consider the lighting when making a room comfortable and relaxing. Most homes do not have fluorescent lights because the unnatural light can strain eyes, which leads stress-inducing environment rather than a relaxing one. Instead, they are likely to incorporate several lower pools of light that give off a softer, more intimate atmosphere than one massive light up above the head. This is why Danes tend to gravitate towards candles lit in several different places. The additional benefit of this approach is that Danes can use scented candles, adding another layer of hygge to their lighting. You can't exactly have a scented lightbulb!

As the stereotypical winter imagery is associated with the evolution of hygge in one specific culture, many people have come to believe that hygge can only be experienced in the winter, and this is simply not true. Hygge is an emotional, inward, and profoundly personal experience. Because of that, its implementation can be worldwide, year-round, and incorporate any person of any size, shape, color, gender, race, and so on. It doesn't matter the weather, your interests, or whether you like to spend most of your time surrounded by people or alone. Hygge means different things to different people, and it is not discriminatory as you can tailor it to suit your personal preferences.

Even so, the Danish experience up to 17 hours of darkness every single day in the shivering depths of their winters. Their average temperatures hover around 32°F. As they spend more time indoors, the main focus of social interaction is indoors rather than outdoors. Frequent gatherings occur at houses for people to enjoy each other's company, and these types of gatherings take place year-round. However, while the gathering of others might stimulate one person, some people will enjoy and seek the silence that solitude brings.

And that is just fine. Hygge is flexible like that.

One of the cruxes of hygge is 'being kind to yourself.' Although that phrase may be overused, it couldn't be more accurate in the hygge context. Hygge means indulging in something that truly allows you to settle down, quit rushing around your day stressed and anxious, and enjoy what life offers you in more comfortable moments. For some, hygge is a hot tub and a glass of wine. For others, hygge is a late-night binge-watch of their favorite television show. For others, it is dinner and drinks out with friends. And for some individuals, it is wrapping up in a blanket or dancing alone to music. All of these situations can be considered hygge. Not matter what time of day or year, the person—and not the circumstance—always dictates what hygge is. And the circumstance is up to the individual to manipulate to allow them the best possible chance of experiencing hygge.

In Denmark and Danish culture in general, self-enforced deprivation is hardly a thing, especially when compared to Western cultures. Rather than refusing to eat certain comfort foods or refusing alcoholic drinks, many Danes encourage indulging in these luxuries of life rather than abstaining from them. But they do preach moderation, not just infinite consumption. Why? Because low levels of indulgence can lower stress levels and reduce random cravings. Practicing moderation can also prevent overindulgence. Many people believe that allowing oneself consistently to indulge in relaxation will result in obesity. Yet, the highest-dieting country in the world is the United States, and it consistently remains the number one country globally for obesity rates, with a whopping 34% of the population considered morbidly obese.

With its intentional indulging for hygge purposes and comfort, Denmark has a significantly lower 19% of its population classified as obese, with 7% overall considered morbidly obese. This statistic is still a problem, of course, but the Danes have far less of a problem than their American counterparts do.

Therefore, these statistics do not match the countries' frames of mind regarding promotion of indulgence, which you may find ironic.

Let's explore this further.

Just as the prohibition era in the United States saw a significant rise in alcohol consumption, forced restriction causes an overindulgence of foods, libations, and entertainment. When the American government abolished prohibition, alcohol consumption levels began to level out, and the percentage of people treated for alcoholism plummeted. Why? Because there was no longer legally enforced deprivation going on. People had more of a choice, rather than a suppressed desire. If we suppress our urges too much, they can manifest in extreme and self-destructive ways. Therefore, it is essential that we cut ourselves a bit of a break and ensure we live a life of moderation and leeway. Unless it is absolutely fundamental to cut something from your life entirely, like it is for an alcoholic who attends Alcoholics Anonymous and admits they are powerless against the substance, moderation is generally a healthy way to engage in hygge.

There's a basic psychological phenomenon called the "pleasure principle." It is a Freudian concept that hygge feeds off. The idea centers on the fact that our base functions (sex, hunger, thirst, and anger) must always be met. They are the biological basis for any human being. By refusing to fulfill those desires, we breed anxiety, tension, and stress, leading to an outpouring of indulgence in our basic desires. Hygge encourages the idea of indulging in pleasures every day to fulfill those basic urges, so the stress and anxiety never build. When forced deprivation begins to happen, tensions mount, and the idea of "binging and purging" begins to rear its ugly head because the guilt associated with indulging in it can overtake the soul—and this is especially true if the behavior is illegal!

In a state of hygge, the person lives a life that gives the body exactly what it needs but goes deeper than just nutrition. Therefore, for hygge, we should seek to satiate not only our stomachs and bodies but also nurture our souls with high-quality, comfort-inducing food and drink.

Remember, you should feel and experience hygge rather than identify it. The experience of hygge varies from person to person and is partially dependent on what tends to breed anxiety and stress within a particular individual. For some, indulging in a sweet treat at the end of the day can foster a sense of peace. A long walk in the early morning hours to watch the sunrise gives some people the ability to breathe deeply and smile. And for others still, the mere idea of locking themselves away and turning the light off to lay in the darkness is their comfort and makes them feel secure. Neither approach is correct per se, but each approach has the potential to be hygge for any given person. That's the magic of it!

Again, what any person deems hygge depends on how something makes them feel. What one person calls relaxing, another calls a nuisance. What one person considers safe; another considers uninteresting. What one person considers indulgent; another might find disgusting. The beauty of hygge is the beauty of life—every individual is different, and no two experiences are the same.

A way to picture this can be to envision the music you like. Perhaps you like heavy metal, but someone else likes hip hop, whereas someone else likes jazz. Each of these genres could create hygge in specific individuals but could actively work against an experience of hygge in others.

Therefore, hygge is so much more than merely understanding the origins and how it is labeled. It goes way beyond a mere ideal within the Danish culture. The stereotypical images we have associated with hygge and its lifestyle may be elements born out of one particular culture on the planet during a specific time of year, but hygge is more than even the sum of these images. Hygge can span every holiday, season, weekday, hour of the day, geography, and mood. The only thing it is dependent upon is the person implementing the lifestyle, and that lifestyle only has one rule: experience the comfort and safety that life can afford.

CHAPTER 2:

FUNDAMENTALS OF HYGGE

I t can be challenging to understand the fundamentals of hygge because the concept tailors to the individual. It can be even more challenging to pin down the fundamentals because hygge does not have a step-by-step guide. It is the deep-felt necessity of relaxing our souls, allowing us to cast aside our worries and enjoy something that fills a present need for our emotional and mental well-being. However, there are a few things to keep in mind when initiating hygge, no matter the season or the person adopting the lifestyle. Therefore, despite hygge's individualistic nature, you can still use some foundational tools in your quest to develop hygge in your life more effectively.

Although the words "warm" and "cozy" are often overused when discussing hygge, they still fit better than most terms. With hygge, no matter what you are enjoying, comfort and pleasure are paramount. This idea—one that has been trending on social media platforms such as Pinterest and Twitter—has the foundation of nurturing one's emotional and mental well-being. If someone is consciously indulging in hygge, it is imperative to feel these two things. When there is comfort, there is relaxation; when there is pleasure, there is happiness. These two ideals combined create the ultimate bodily conditions for reducing stress and alleviating anxieties, which lowers cortisol levels, leaving the body to rest and heal in ways it so desperately needs. Therefore, the first fundamental in incorporating hygge into your life is to consider what makes you feel warm on the inside and cozy on the outside.

The Danes splice the word "hygge" when labeling things that contribute towards the lifestyle specifically. For example, "sweatpants," or other pants someone would never wear in public but will frequently wear around the house, are called "hyggebukser." The word "hyggelig" is also used relatively often in Danish culture, and this word simply means "hygge-like." Another spliced Danish word is "hyggekrog," which refers to an area of the home where a person can hunker down and relax. These words are spliced with the word "hygge" because they have evolved into Denmark's own "basics" for living, contributing to a hygge lifestyle.

To implement hygge for the first time, you will have to do so consciously. When you navigate through the world, including within your own house, consider what aspects of your day or what areas you feel are the coziest and most pleasurable. Begin to make a mental checklist as to what you think hygge is to you. In these early stages, you could perhaps even write down the things that feel hygge to you. Doing so may reinforce the necessary behaviors for you to implement the lifestyle for your betterment.

While Danes find hygge effortless to employ, other cultures—especially fast-paced ones like American culture—require individuals to make a conscious effort to slow down to really take in life's finer moments and pleasures. Therefore, Americans should employ a "conscious effort" when laying the foundation of a hygge lifestyle. When you get more in tune with thinking about what hygge is and what it isn't, you will likely implement hygge more naturally in your life and will no longer have to make that mental or physical checklist.

When cultures prize speed-of-light communication and hard work over personal well-being and familial connection, a rift can happen among the fundamental aspects of human health: mental, emotional, spiritual, and physical. Food has to be served fast, coffee has to be fast, meetings have to be fast, and work has to be fast. Then, people return home, and television has to be fast, the internet has to be fast, and sleep has to be fast. There is little room for slowing down if you comply too deeply with American and other Western societies' cultural pressures.

These efforts at meeting a perceived "need for speed" only wreak havoc on the body to the detriment of its health. Never slowing down increases the risk of chemical dependencies (such as caffeine) and increases the risk of various health issues. Denmark is the third healthiest country in the world, while countries like the United States and the United Kingdom are among the 10 unhealthiest countries in the world. But why is this the case? Part of the reason is the way the cultures prioritize family and well-being alongside work. If work becomes the top priority, health falls to the wayside. If family, friends, and personal experience become the most important aspects of someone's life, they will likely live healthier and happier lifestyles. It really is that simple.

This is why people in countries that prioritize work over health will need to make conscious efforts at first in order to implement the hygge lifestyle. It requires a refocusing of priorities, a relearning, if you will. If an individual implements hygge for long enough and reaps the scientifically proven benefits, then a conscious effort will no longer be required.

But in order to reach this state of unconscious application of hygge, an individual must complete the difficult task of laying the foundation. After all, you can't build a functioning house without a solid foundation, can you?

Another critical aspect of hygge is the application of togetherness—for some at least, because others enjoy spending their downtime alone. Many natural introverts, especially those with chaotic jobs, enjoy coming home and just being alone in solitude. So, while many will say that "togetherness" is a component of hygge, it might not be so for others. The Danish culture has integrated togetherness for various reasons, including having larger families, an emphasis on familial bonding, and the harsh weather they experience, which brings collective enjoyment into the comfort of people's homes, but that does not mean "togetherness" is a requirement for hygge. However, instead of "togetherness," peaceful "enjoyment" is a fundamental aspect of hygge. In other words, if you enjoy your solitude and seek it out more than you seek out group activities, then so be it! Spend more time in solitude and embrace this as a fundamental aspect of your hygge.

In order to be relaxed, comfortable, and content, the person implementing the hygge lifestyle simply needs to enjoy what they are doing. For many, this means gathering friends and family together around a great big table of food while laughing and telling stories. For others, that type of crowd and noise level may increase their worries and stresses, and they might want to be excused as soon as possible so they can go back to their personal spaces and enjoy their version of hygge. And some will even enjoy both of these things and find hygge in social gatherings and solitude!

Remember that solitude is different than loneliness. The former involves self-imposed exile from people in order to decompress, and the latter is a perpetual state of sadness arising from the absence of people someone feels care about them. One has the potential to be very hygge; the other is the exact opposite. If you are lonely, it is great to reach out to people you care about and care about you. This type of reaching out will surely lead you to feel more comfortable and will allow you to experience hygge more easily. Therefore, fundamentally, hygge can be the presence of people or the absence of people. It all depends on how you feel.

In order to understand the fundamentals of hygge, it is crucial to understand what hygge is not. Hygge is not something you must feel compelled to do at all costs, especially to the point that it bothers you if you are not engaging in something you consider hygge. If it feels forced or required of you in some fashion, you will likely not feel relaxed or comfortable—thus defeating the primary purpose of a hygge lifestyle in the first place. Just like a homework assignment is required, or the due date for a paper is mandatory, that will induce stress. Even if you want something as simple as a meal with a specific calorie count, that meal can become stressful. Something as basic as choosing what to eat can be just another thing that you have to remember and measure out to the point of stress. Remember that too many self-imposed rules will not allow you to feel hygge and will likely be detrimental to your overall wellbeing. Even what would have otherwise been a "relaxing" family dinner can become yet another block of time that you spend feeling stressed.

Therefore, you must look at hygge as something you choose to do, and never as a requirement. You should intentionally seek it out for the purpose of goodness, comfort, and coziness, and give yourself a break if you think you're doing something that isn't "hygge-like."

Other ways to experience hygge are to get out and experience something entirely new. Many people find hygge within adventures and thrill-seeking activities, but they may not have realized these things were hygge for them until they tried them out. Part of hygge is not only falling back onto things you understand about yourself; it is also about discovering aspects about yourself you did not previously know. Maybe you will take that hike up the mountain and realize it's not your cup of tea, but now you know for sure. Perhaps you will decide to take your best friend and go skydiving and realize the sensation of free-falling is more relaxing for you than you realized it would be! Or perhaps there's an international cuisine you've never tried because you've always assume you will not like it. Perhaps it is time to try that Indian curry, or that pad Thai, or those dragon fruits you always eye at the market but never end up getting.

In short, you are never going to know what you find and do not find hygge until you actively try. You might even surprise yourself, so be ready to be open to all experiences!

When most people first implement hygge, they stick to what they know. But do not think for one second that hygge is simply about staying within those boundaries. Living a hygge lifestyle is also about branching out and pushing beyond your comfort zones to discover who you really are. The person who enjoys warm nights indoors on cold winter evenings might also enjoy bundling up and taking a crisp morning walk to watch the sunrise. But if they never do it, they will never know the extent to which their hygge lifestyle could expand. Therefore, experimentation and openness to new experiences can be fundamental to a hygge lifestyle. Give new things a try!

The "fundamentals" of living a hygge lifestyle are impossible to separate from how the person implementing it feels. It is all about how the concepts, starting points, and experiences trigger emotions and states of relaxation. The basics of a hygge lifestyle will always remain emotional. It is a lifestyle that is inherently shaped by the person living it, and no list of rules or commands will genuinely capture it. If an experience conjures negative emotions and a feeling of discomfort, it does not matter that the person next to them is enjoying it. To them, it will never be hygge. And that is fine. Hygge will always feel and mean different things to different people. Therefore, it is impossible to come up with a one-size-fits-all approach to the fundamentals of hygge.

All hygge fundamentals are truly individual, and it is—although potentially unsatisfying to hear—up to you to determine what the fundamentals of hygge are for you. As long as you're comfortable and giving yourself an adequate amount of winding down time and pleasure, then you're likely acting in line with a hygge way of life.

CHAPTER 3:

BENEFITS OF THE HYGGE LIFESTYLE

There are many different benefits to leading the type of lifestyle hygge offers. For many, reducing stress and all of the related health complications is paramount. However, for others, it will impact them in other ways, even though it still may offer more covert medical benefits. As with many different facets of hygge, the way the lifestyle will benefit an individual will vary. Although there are no specific benefits that all will share, some general benefits will apply to most people. So, let's get on to exploring precisely some of the benefits the hygge lifestyle can bring, and what you could do potentially to bring about those benefits.

The Danes—as well as other people from the Nordic regions—use a high-form of hygge that requires significant time spent outdoors, especially wandering through nature. Time in nature allows an individual to take in the natural beauty around them, unplug and get away from their electronics, and get the body and mind much-needed exercise by moving through and thriving in the space of a natural environment. Going outside and exercising is a healthy routine that will lead to a more satisfied, and more hygge, lifestyle. Many studies have shown that exercising outdoors, even with just a leisurely walk, can bring about more benefits than working out in a gym. If you can get up and get out, then do so, because it can bring about hygge and help you in times of need. It will get you in the right frame of mind for further hygge in your day.

Sometimes, when you are inside and trying to problem-solve, you can be too close to a problem, get frustrated, and not come up with a solution. However, if you get outside to change your surroundings and get your body moving, you will likely be able to develop solutions as you allow your subconscious mind to do some of the work you were trying too hard to assign to your conscious mind. Be sure to bring adequate water, food, and even a notepad when you go outdoors for an extended period of time. You can even bring your hygge comforts that lead to further benefits from engaging in this activity!

Hunting is another popular pastime in Danish culture. Being out in nature is synonymous with the clearing of one's head and leaving worries behind, as well as ensuring a meal is sourced in the wilderness and not merely bought in a market. Hunting engages and strengthens many different traits: composure, control, accuracy, patience, stillness, and respect for nature. However, hunting isn't for everyone, especially if you are a vegetarian or a vegan. In this case, you could perhaps learn how to forage and pick berries, fruits, and mushrooms. However, be sure you know exactly what you're doing when it comes to foraging—there are plenty of poisonous things out in nature!

If working hard and breaking a sweat in nature does not sound relaxing, simply being amidst it with only birdsong and a breeze passing through leaves to accompany you while you breathe in the outdoor air deeply can also be hygge-like. The outside air is crisper than it is inside your home, and, while it might be better filtered, pollution of the air in most homes is higher than it is outside. This means that "getting fresh air" can stimulate the brain in ways staying inside cannot, and this can be a real benefit that helps increase your levels of hygge.

Another significant benefit of hygge is what happens when stress levels in the body drop. Cortisol is the chemical usually associated with stress, but it has a broader impact on the body. It is a life-sustaining chemical that secretes from the adrenal gland and moderates a host of bodily functions. Blood sugar levels, metabolism, blood pressure, and immune responses are just a few of our bodies' vital components that cortisol influences directly. Cortisol naturally fluctuates as our body needs it to, regulating everything from blood vessel constriction to the leveling of sugars in the blood. With a fast-paced lifestyle, the body does not have a chance to return to a "normal state" before cortisol has to kick in and regulate something back down to normal.

These harmful cortisol levels can lead to a host of medical issues, which can worsen if the adrenal glands become fatigued because they can no longer keep up with the cortisol production necessary to regulate the bodily systems. This can result in sleep disruption, decreased bone density, blood sugar imbalances, and even reduced muscle mass. Not only that, but cortisol latches onto abdominal fats, securing them to their positions, which brings on a host of other medical issues. In essence, it is vital to regulate our cortisol levels by alleviating the stresses in our lives, something which a hygge way of living is excellent for.

Cortisol also contributes to the shortening of our telomeres, which ages our bodies faster. Telomeres are what protect our genetic information and sit at the end of our linear chromosomes. Have you ever thought about why world leaders seem to age so quickly when they take office? That's usually because of the high stress levels that affect their telomere lengths. Telomere reduction leads to aging skin and grey hair and affects an individual's lifespan. The more we control our cortisol through hygge-like techniques, the slower our telomeres will shorten as a result of stress.

From a biological standpoint, then, hygge is simply a moment where the reduction of stress and stressful outside influences improve overall health. Using hygge allows the body's cortisol levels to drop, allowing the body to regulate itself back to normal. If an individual indulges in hygge consistently, then the body has a chance to heal from some of the internal damage cortisol tends to inflict.

These couple of benefits alone increase the happiness someone experiences because the brain's chemical reactions are not being intruded upon by a constant surge of cortisol. Keep this in check, and work on how to release the brain's own feel-good chemicals like dopamine, serotonin, and oxytocin.

While there is a lot of emphasis on what is 'natural' within the Danish culture's interpretation of hygge, the simple fact is that the most significant benefit to this lifestyle is its lack of fundamental rules, as we explored in the previous chapter. Remember, being hygge is based on how you feel internally at any given moment, especially when you have unplugged from electronics, put away work, and found ways to unwind and de-stress. That being said, technology can also be used for hygge, especially if you love gaming, music, or film. It all depends on how you use it and the feeling that it invokes within you.

Therefore, the hygge lifestyle can be tailored to suit anyone. Some can find their hygge moments out at a club dancing in a crowd, while others will enjoy being alone and curled up on their sofa reading a good book. Both are hygge moments that can be found within wildly separate worlds simply based on how the person feels. The benefits an individual will get from these moments will determine whether their actions are hygge or not.

The lifestyle of hygge and what it promotes can also ward off certain mental illnesses. People who struggle with seasonal depression, drastic mood swings, and feelings of anxiousness have reported that making hygge their new way of life helps them regulate their symptoms. Through hygge, many have lowered their medication dosages, and a few have decided to come off their medications altogether. As hygge promotes a better lifestyle when it comes to individual health and focuses on being kinder to oneself, people often find they can deal with mental illness with newfound strength. This confidence can eliminate unnecessary feelings of guilt that can cause anxiety, halting an individual's negative carousel of thoughts. In this context, you could even call hygge a wonder-drug!

A fundamental fact of hygge is the absence of stress, but if you are in a stressful situation and cannot relieve yourself of it, hygge can then be utilized to deal with the stress more successfully. For example, you are already 10 minutes late for your workday, but you know you cannot give up that morning cup of coffee if you expect to be useful. So, when you drive to your favorite coffee shop, a hygge move could be spending $1.00 more to get a larger size and add your favorite flavor. You are likely to feel better about the extra indulgence, and you can relax knowing that you allowed yourself some additional comfort. Of course, this action might make you later, but it also might make you more productive. All you need to do is apologize for your lack of punctuality and even make light of it to coworkers. We're all late every now and then, and it's okay to slip up sometimes. At moments in which you think you've made a mistake, let yourself know it's okay to so you can move on. The hygge mindset will allow you to forgive yourself, as the feelings of guilt will otherwise get in the way of comfort. Remember, hygge can alleviate stress, so use it to help you calm down whenever you need to!

The benefits that come with a hygge lifestyle are not merely emotional; they are medical. Adopting the lifestyle that Danes consider a natural way of life has turned the lives of thousands of individuals around, and it is all because they decided to live outside of their own culture's norm. However, you may still not be quite sure how to apply hygge to your own life.

And for that, there is an answer.

CHAPTER 4:

APPLYING HYGGE TO YOUR LIFE

With hygge being such an interpersonal and reflective experience, outlining exactly how to apply its exacting aspects is near-impossible. I can give you examples and flesh out some scenarios, but remember the fundamental tenet of hygge: only the emotion it elicits from the person experiencing it gives hygge its meaning. Therefore, there is a lot you need to work out for yourself when it comes to applying hygge to your life. However, there are still tips and methods you can learn to help you along the way, and that's what this chapter is all about.

Many people who want to start implementing the hygge lifestyle say they feel rushed in their day-to-day life. The terms "stressed," "overworked," and "not enough time" frequently come up in conversation between people in Western countries like the US and the UK, and it is the pressure of this fast-paced lifestyle that makes them want a change in their lives.

At the very least, these people want to find a way to abate some of the stresses during their everyday lives. Western culture usually focuses on what's next, and many people find it difficult to wind down properly. Some take their work home, and some stay in their offices so late they only just have time to get home, eat dinner, sleep, and go straight back to work again. To apply hygge into your everyday life, you must spot the patterns of rushing around too much, trying to cram too many stressful things into one day, and give your body and mind the room to relax and unwind.

For many of us, vacations are full of hygge. On vacation, we tend to focus on relaxation, comfort, indulgence, and a slower pace. We also tend to surround ourselves with people whose company we enjoy. Maybe someone else has taken that vacation alone to experience the solitude life has to offer, in which case they are still relaxed, stress-free, and indulging in life's basic pleasures. For many, hygge is a simpler lifestyle, not because that quality is a requirement, but because modern life has become too hectic and complicated. Many of us are bombarded with constant alerts, notifications, and distractions. The lifestyle encouraged by hygge is one in which you implement the pleasures of vacations into your day-to-day life.

We might be used to electronics buzzing in our pockets or dinging on our dinner tables, but we are not relaxed around them. Those sounds quickly become associated with meetings, homework, angry bosses, last-minute assignments, and even domestic emergencies. These beeps and constant phone calls are not relaxing because our internal electrical signals have associated these sounds with emergencies and urgent messages. They cause a spike in our adrenaline, raise stress levels, and increase our heartrates. They work against what we seek to achieve with hygge!

Only when we relieve ourselves of these alerts and notifications can we begin to relax. There are many things we can do to achieve this peace and quiet. We can start by turning off our phones when we are outside of work hours. There's no need to allow everyone to contact you at all hours of the day and for you to always be available. You need that essential hygge time that'll allow you to unwind and enjoy life. Who wants to be twenty minutes through an engrossing movie only for someone to send you a work email that you could just as quickly answer the next day and not in the precious hours of an evening you're trying to enjoy?

The classical definition of psychological conditioning is a principle that makes hygge easier to implement. You may know this term from the behaviorist Ivan Pavlov's dogs with the bells experiment, where he conditioned dogs' mouths to salivate at the sound of bells because he would ring the bells whenever he brought them food. The result was that whenever he rang the bell, the dogs' mouths would start to salivate even without food.

We can use this conditioning on ourselves to get us to relax more and live the hygge lifestyle. You can condition yourself to feel hygge as much as your notification bells have likely conditioned you to feel anxiety or dread. Let's say you work from home, and your living room and your office happen to be the same room. You might, therefore, need to make changes to your room and condition yourself into relaxation. Once your workday ends, and you shut down your work computer, perhaps put a specific candle on, or change the lighting. These sensory signals can help you pair a smell or sight with relaxation, and you will be able to separate your workday from your at-home relaxation. Perhaps you could do the same by going outside for a walk as soon as your workday ends. You could even have a small reminder that pops up on your computer screen that it's time to get up and finish your day and go for a stroll. Or to play and follow a yoga video. Whatever it is that relaxes you and helps you find your hygge!

If you do not know what inherently relaxes you, then starting with a few basics can help. For example, try lying on your bed with the light on, and then turn it off. Did the light off make you feel panicked, even if a little bit? If so, darkness might not mean hygge for you. If you feel too exposed with the light on, then maybe the light is not hygge for you. If neither the light on nor off elicited any sort of response, then experiment with different types of lights. Try a group of lit candles or a machine that casts colorful patterns on the ceiling. Try using lightbulbs for which you can change the color with a remote. Try adhering glow-in-the-dark stickers to something in your room. Experimentation is your friend here. Sometimes it isn't the lighting, but the room that promotes a specific feeling, so you could even try the experiment in another room. Hygge goes further than an emotional experience. It is a creative experience, and you can find novel ways to shift your environments to produce a hygge-like experience within you.

Pay attention to how your body reacts to things like lighting, smells, the temperature of the room, coziness and comfort, music, and anything else you can think of. The more you pay attention to engaging your senses in the best possible way, the closer you will get to discovering your inner hygge. And don't feel bad if you don't work it out right away; you will get there in time. There's no need to rush—be hygge about it!

For some, slipping into hygge gradually is necessary. Drastic and significant changes make some people anxious, and that defeats the point of hygge. If you are someone who struggles with rapid change, then be sure to implement new techniques more slowly so you can get used to it. The point of applying hygge to your life is to abate and dwindle those adverse and emotional knee-jerk reactions to things to bring about more bliss and other positive emotions. So, try a few simple things at a time: keep your favorite candy at your desk at work, or purchase a travel coffee mug with your favorite color or design on it to hold your coffee in the mornings. If you are someone who enjoys colorful or mismatched socks, consider wearing them underneath your clothes. Even though others might not see them, you will know they are there, and they might make you smile. The point with these types of deliberate implementation of hygge-like actions is that they can all contribute to the overall purpose and experience of hygge.

A smaller gesture is taking two more minutes in the bathroom to sit and breathe in the stall. Maybe you are not ready to implement colorful coffee mugs and mismatched socks that make you smile. Perhaps you long for a couple of minutes to yourself where someone is not trying to get in touch with you. If that is the case, then use your bathroom breaks at work or home to accomplish this. Slip into the bathroom, leave your phone behind, and sit for a more extended period of time. Take in deep breaths through your nose and close your eyes. Relish the fact that no one is calling your name, and you do not have to answer to anyone but yourself.

But perhaps you want a bit of social interaction at work. If your work has a kitchen, then maybe go there and make some coffee or tea and talk to anyone else that is doing the same thing. Perhaps you could even offer hot drinks to others around you. You'll be doing something nice for people, and you'll get to be in the kitchen longer than you would have anticipated originally!

Sometimes these types of hygge-like moments are all someone needs to abate their stress hormones and push them back down to a healthier level. Anything that will help you relax, be it at home, in the car, or at work, will bring about more of a hygge mindset. When facing stress or decisions, perhaps ask yourself, "What is the most hygge-like thing I can do right now?" And you'll likely start making decisions that will help you be more relaxed and satisfied in the future.

Many people also wonder about hygge-style foods. Foods that are considered "comfort-inducing" are, almost always, synonymous with "unhealthy" and "fattening." People wonder if that type of thing can lead to an unhealthy lifestyle that eventually brings the opposite of what they want to experience.

Hygge is not a lifestyle of overindulgence. Just as never relieving stress is toxic for the body, overindulging brings about a different type of toxicity. In this regard, the hygge lifestyle, when it comes to food, can be described as "a break." Living a healthy lifestyle and making sure your body is taken care of is of utmost importance. However, allowing yourself a double-scooped ice cream cone every now and again may be right for you. If you turn your back on everyday pleasures all the time, you likely do not have a hygge-like relationship with food and yourself. Give yourself a break. If you follow the hygge lifestyle adequately, it will not lead to unhealthy habits; it is the lack of self-control that leads to a lifestyle to no longer be hygge-like.

Food has a more prominent role to play than mere consumption and its associated benefits. You may find that cooking, baking, and plating up a satisfying meal rewarding. Some may consider measuring and controlling the exact ingredients in recipes relaxing and comforting. In contrast, many others may feel the act of eating half of the cake batter before it even hits the pan hygge. Some people enjoy putting the food on a plate in an aesthetically pleasing manner, and even more people enjoy cooking meals and then taking them to someone else to enjoy. The hygge possibilities with food are endless, so do not stop at the mere consumption of it. If you haven't learned to cook yet, but you've always wanted to, then why not start now? You can try cooking simpler foods like pesto pasta or any other simple favorites you might have. If you're exceedingly confident, perhaps you could even share your meals with others. Your possibilities with food really are endless, and you can start finding out what flavors go well together, what spices go well with what vegetables, and which wine complements a specific cheese!

If you wonder if there is a specific percentage of hygge that has to be found each day for you to be living a hygge lifestyle, you run the risk of having a Dane chuckle at you. A complicated emotional feeling goes way beyond any attempt to take something and boil it down to statistical analysis. No, hygge isn't something you can measure or see on a pie chart because it's way more individual than that. You can fill your day with as little or as much hygge as you desire, and it is up to you how satisfied you feel with the outcome.

However, for those who do not feel self-aware enough or do not enjoy experiencing deep and potentially intense swells of emotion, hygge is hard to implement and understand. For Danes, hygge is something that they practice every day. From the chimney sweepers to the mayors of their biggest cities, hygge is a regular part of the well-being of the person experiencing it.

And the fact that it spans social classes and people from all walks of life might make hygge seem mind-boggling. But rest assured, it is a straightforward wide-ranging philosophy and way of living.

Applying hygge to one's life is like starting any new habit: at first, it has to be intentional, and it will likely feel foreign. Sometimes it has to go on calendars or in someone's phone reminders, and sometimes people even have to write it on a sheet of paper and pin it to their refrigerator or above their desk. Either way, the constant reminder will be helpful to making hygge second nature. Although many people would think this defeats the purpose of hygge, in a society that runs on the ingrained impulse of "constant" activity, scheduling "downtime" is almost necessary to make it happen. In other words, intentionality and planning can help you live a hygge lifestyle and not be detrimental to it.

Like any habit, hygge will work its way into the daily routine of the person implementing it, and if it holds any sway or value in their lives, they will make time for it. Even though some days might make hygge more challenging to implement, having a few methods to keep the lifestyle a priority will be more useful than implanting no hygge principles one day and loads of hygge principles the next. Like keeping in touch with a best friend or checking up on a beloved neighbor, hygge will become more of a habit the more you work it into a daily routine, and it will end up becoming something to look forward to rather than a difficult challenge to overcome. The more you focus your mind on creating hygge experiences and cultivating precisely what that looks like and means to you, the more quickly it will become second nature. You won't even have to think about it, and you will essentially become an honorary Dane!

Therefore, the true application of hygge is when it becomes second nature. Remember to practice it daily and as much as possible, and your present and future self will reap the constant rewards and benefits.

However, one rule that is synonymous with hygge is "unplugging." Turning off your phone, shutting down your laptop, and getting off those videoconference calls is imperative to the application of hygge. Sure, it might seem odd for a concept that is supposed to have no definite rules, but there is a physical and medical benefit behind switching off. Therefore, you should probably pay attention to it.

When we spend too long staring at screens, it is unlikely that we are doing so in a good posture or breathing correctly to give our lungs and bodies the vital energy needed for optimal output in any given day. When we breathe correctly and allow our minds to wander, we will likely be happier and more creative. We are all too quick to fill any downtime or any moment of potential boredom—like when one person goes to the bathroom in a restaurant, and the other person instantly takes out their phone—to fully take in the world around us. One word of advice is to turn your phone off at certain times of the day. Perhaps you're at home, and it's after 9 PM, or you're out to a restaurant with a friend or loved one. These are good times to turn your phone off or put on silent and place out of reach. Don't worry, your phone isn't going anywhere. So, unplug in the knowledge that you can look at your social media feeds later!

There are many theories about whether or not the EMF (electromagnetic frequency) signals emitted by our daily bombardment of electronics negatively affect our bodies. However, these theories haven't entirely passed the speculative stage. On the other hand, there have been many conclusive studies performed on what our obsession with technology has done to us and how staring at screens negatively affects our sleep, as we shall discuss.

Our eyes have photoreceptors that prompt the waking up and shutting down of our bodies, and they affect the release of melatonin—a hormone in the pineal gland that tells our bodies that it's time to sleep. Because of these sensitive photoreceptors, it is essential to switch off the lights and electronics early if you want to fall asleep at a suitable time to wake up on time. Our photoreceptors help align our natural circadian rhythms (the inward and natural clock our body runs on) with the outside world. When these signals are activated, specific responses are provoked, and those responses prompt either alertness or sleep to overtake the body.

So, when someone is up and on their phone at 11 PM or watching television in their beds at 1 AM, the light glaring from their electronics will interfere with their regular sleeping patterns. The blue light emitted from these devices blocks the release of melatonin, making it far more difficult to fall asleep. Coupled with this, you should associate your be with sleep and not any other activity. If you are looking at your phone with your back pressed against your mattress, reading a newsfeed, thinking about politics, or any other topic that is likely to induce stress, you will start associating your bed with that type of stress. This stress is not conducive to sleep. For starters, you should set up time earlier in your day to look at these types of things (if at all), and you should also put "worry time" into your schedule.

You might chuckle at the term "worry time," but bear with me—it is a fundamental concept to help you sleep better. When we spend our days switched on, we give our minds little or no time to wonder. By the time we lie down in bed, all the worries and concerns we blocked out using technology throughout the day will surface when we lie down to sleep. If we deal with these concerns earlier, sound sleep will likely come. And sound sleep is hygge—you do not feel your best if you are sleep deprived.

But what are some of the dangers that sleep deprivation can bring?

Sleep deprivation can lead to a host of negative things such as a higher risk for strokes, memory problems, a greater chance of traffic accidents, and even hallucinations. Here is a good lesson Westerners can learn from the Danes—when we sit in our chairs, we do not need to spend hours staring at our phones. Alongside its disruptiveness to our sleep patterns, our harmful postures (we even have the term "text neck" to refer to the lowering of our heads when we stare at our phones too much) also negatively impacts our eyes because we have to strain them when looking at all the small text coming from a bright light. When you disrupt your body's natural circadian rhythm, it will wreak havoc on your sleeping patterns and compromise your health. In short: staring at your phone impacts your life for the worse, and it is also shortening it.

Be more mindful of your technology consumption because overindulgence is nowhere near the ballpark of what hygge means.

If there is any one way to sum up the implementation of hygge accurately, it is this: turn it off, lay it down, and breathe slowly, deeply, mindfully, and through your nose. There is an inherently slow pace to a hygge moment or lifestyle simply because of the fast pace our society seems intent on keeping. From moments that create fond memories to lying in the dark and just existing, you can find hygge in the simplest of places as long it reduces your stress, anxiety, and panic. Getting away from the constant dopamine hits of buzzing and ringing technology is an excellent way to calm your body and mind and relax your way into a hygge state of being.

The hygge lifestyle is rooted in medical reality and psychological principles that form our physical and mental health foundations. Hygge brings to the forefront a self-awareness that serves the medical needs we must understand for the rest of our lives if we are going to live life to the fullest.

Hygge is not a fad, or a trend, or something that will eventually fade into the background. Instead, it is a way of life that promotes good health benefits on a physical, emotional, chemical, and hormonal level. Remember this, and you will find it easier and easier to apply hygge to your life—no matter what the season is.

CHAPTER 5:

HOW HYGGE DIFFERS WITH THE SEASONS

Despite the stereotypical pictures of cabins covered in snow and other images used to represent hygge and its lifestyle in the heart of winter, hygge transcends seasons. As the lifestyle can be tailored to a specific person depending on their emotional and physical state, seasonal changes only serve to promote more hygge-like moments, not diminish them. The changing seasons encourage creativity in finding hygge-like moments even when the environment changes. The typical pictures we tend to see of fuzzy socks, steaming hot cups of spiced apple cider, and groups of flickering candles are all beautiful things, but that is because the lifestyle of hygge is concentrated mainly within just one culture on the planet. So, we are most familiar with how Danish hygge-like moments have manifested in the types of climates and curiosities their country has to offer. However, there are ways to integrate it into your culture.

So, now we know that hygge is not seasonal, although the seasons will affect your implementation of hygge. If you are someone who enjoys long walks on the beach and feeling the sun beat down on your face, it does not mean that having a hygge lifestyle is only possible during the summer. Beaches are open all year long, and in many places in the world, the sun still shines in the winter. If the sun has been gone a few days, consider traveling to a place where the sun is shining, or perhaps even indulge in a low-light tanning session. If you are someone who enjoys knee-high socks, large blankets, and hot mugs of apple cider, then your hygge is not only possible in the wintertime. You could sit outside at dawn, or crank the air conditioning, or sit in the basement, dress warmly, bundle up under a throw blanket, and make your favorite hot drink while you watch a movie. Even so, you can still use the seasons to find your own hygge in other ways. Sure, you may prefer winter, but that doesn't mean you have to spend all the other seasons longing for it. Find things you enjoy in the heat as well as things you enjoy in the cold. Doing so will maximize your chances of experiencing hygge year-round!

For many people, hygge is a way to get through the more challenging seasons. It is a way of finding comfort during a time that could otherwise be full of discomfort. Seasonal affective disorder, also known as seasonal depression, affects millions of people every season, from summer to winter and back again. However, it typically comes on during the winter months of the year due to the lack of sunlight. Sunlight is responsible for giving our bodies vitamin D, and when it is weak, tucked behind the clouds, and cold out, we are not going to get enough of it. Many of us do not think to take vitamin D supplements because we do not realize that vitamin D plays a major role in balancing chemicals throughout the brain. When your brain is starved for something that makes it stable, it becomes unstable. This instability can lead to difficult symptoms such as fatigue, depression, brain fog, and malnutrition. A lack of vitamin D can wreak havoc on the body's metabolism, disabling it from drawing the nutrients out of the food it needs in order for the body to function properly. People report decreased appetites with low vitamin D levels, sluggish behavior, stiff and aching joints, and even chronic headaches.

These types of symptoms are why part of the hygge lifestyle focuses on nutrition. Ensuring you get what nutrients you need, no matter the time of year, means your body and mind will be kept fully functioning. This type of bodily care is essential to one's mental state, which holds a great deal of influence over the physical body's responses. If the mind is suffering from a chemical imbalance that results in depression, a lack of appetite can create issues such as malnutrition, dehydration, and muscular tissue degeneration. If the depression is causing someone to eat constantly, then the rapid weight gain can result in a higher risk for strokes, heart conditions, bone fractures, and osteoporosis.

The importance of the body's physical health is paramount. Therefore, you should utilize the nutritional supplements available to you and introduce hygge into your world, which can help quell the debilitating issues that surface due to seasonal affective disorders. The more you spend time seeking the comfort hygge can offer you, the less likely you are to suffer from mental, emotional, and physical ailments due to seasonal changes. For many, supplementing the lack of vitamin D and eating healthy during the autumn and winter months helps with their seasonal depression. For those who experience it in the spring and summer, attending to things such as allergies and getting tested for allergic reactions, various pollens may help you understand why seasons affect you the way they do.

Furthermore, winter might make it difficult to exercise because it may be too cold outside. Therefore, it might be a good idea to find exercises you can do indoors, be it yoga, workout videos, or your own routines that you make up. Exercising releases necessary endorphins and hormones that will help keep you in high spirits through any season, but especially in winter!

However, know that seasonal affective disorder is different for every person, and utilizing some of these methods does not mean it will dissipate fully. For some, seasonal affective disorder is merely about coping with a season they do not enjoy. If someone does not like the snow or the hot summer months because the temperature of the environment or traveling conditions are not ideal, they can become stressed. This induction of stress can wreak havoc on the body and someone's ability to function with their job, family, and friends. Therefore, not only does it affect the individual, it can cause people who live with or around the sufferer a great deal of hardship.

For the above reason alone, the implementation of hygge throughout all seasons is imperative because it can combat some of these issues that many of us face year-round.

As discussed, winter is the season when most people suffer from low moods. Keeping the body at a comfortable temperature while it is cold outside is ideal for reducing the amount of stress the body is under. Therefore, using heaters, fires, wearing extra layers, warm socks, drinking hot drinks, and having hot showers and baths can all contribute to the experience of hygge. However, these are not the only things considered hygge during those winter months. Watching a movie with a friend, staying in bed longer during a day off from work, and sitting still and breathing mindfully are also considered hygge. They help relieve stress and will give the body a chance to repair itself from the stress of a day-to-day routine.

Other activities that can help in the winter months are extended conversations with a good friend, belly laughter over jokes, and watching a great movie in your favorite pair of pajamas. Remember, you do not just have to implement hygge in a social context; it merely has to serve its purpose of de-stressing you. Alone or in a group, you can always find moments to implement more of it.

In the spring months, hygge can come in a variety of forms. Many people enjoy walking through fields of freshly bloomed flowers, and many enjoy going on leisurely nature walks through their neighborhoods after the cold winter months melt into memory. Many enjoy being able to bring out shorts, dresses, and other loose-fitting clothing, and others find peace sitting on their porches and watching the wind blow through the spring trees as they inhale the sweet scent of grass. Spring is a time for growth, and this can be a necessary mindset when it comes to ensuring that your spring is full of hygge and hygge-like moments.

However, some people struggle with seasonal allergies during times of bloom, so inhaling a bunch of pollen and plant dander may not be ideal. These allergies may cause some people to stay inside more of the days and to shut their windows from the outside air, which others would deem fresh. Even so, it is still possible to be hygge in the springtime. For one, going to see a doctor and getting some answers and medications for your allergies can be hygge in and of itself because not only can it provide solutions, it can give relief from allergic reactions allowing a sufferer to more fully enjoy all that spring has to offer. Even long showers to wash off that irritating pollen can be hygge, as can going on a drive through the countryside rather than a walk. Many wooded areas and mountainous terrain trails have alternate routes for cars, and the views are spectacular. You can take the drive with friends to create memories or drive alone to secure some peaceful time for yourself. Either way, drive carefully and be mindful of your surroundings to give yourself the best possible hygge experience!

No matter what you decide to do in the springtime, it is hygge as long as you care for your health, reduce your anxiety levels, and treat yourself to something that makes you smile.

Hygge in the summer months is what many people look forward to. For many, beach trips, long and barefoot walks over the sand, swimming in lakes, hiking through a forest, and even tanning are just a few of the ways the summer months can bring about relaxation and hygge. Many enjoy wide-brimmed hats, sitting out in the sun, and drinking an ice-cold beverage. Others enjoy the familial activities that tend to come with the summer months, like picnics and backyard barbecues. However, some people do not have close relationships with their families or do not enjoy the beach, which is perfectly okay. There are other things summer can provide that will give you the full hygge experience.

For example, if you do not enjoy the heat, swimming pools might fit your fancy when it comes to unwinding and relaxing. Maybe lounging around the house in grungy shorts, a baggy t-shirt, and pouring an ice-cold drink is more your style. Perhaps you do not enjoy the beach at all but do enjoy the dizzying heights of the mountains. Going to the mountains during the summer can be perfect for two reasons: 1) the mountains are always a few degrees cooler because of their higher elevation, and 2) the colors of the trees, flowers, and greenery are in full bloom. It makes for beautiful pictures and a serene environment packed with the sounds of nature, wild animals, and a lovely summer breeze. Make sure you keep your distance from the wild animals, though, and never feed them. It is essential not to meddle in nature's affairs as you marvel at it.

In the mountains, like most places, you have options. You can take friends or family, or you can go by yourself. Whichever sounds more comforting and rids you of the anxieties of everyday life will always be the preferred method when leading a hygge lifestyle. You can hike to get some much-needed exercise or drive through the open countryside to enjoy the majestic views. Either way, it is up to you what you do in the mountains. You can even go to a campground and stay for a night or a weekend. You can then fully experience the mountains and unplug from your everyday life.

Finally, we can think about hygge in autumn (fall). Especially in the US, autumn brings about holidays like Halloween and Thanksgiving and even Oktoberfest events inspired by Germany. There are so many things that make people smile and jump for joy during this season: hot apple ciders, pumpkin pies, familial celebrations around tables of food, and the leaves changing into all sorts of exotic colors. Hot temperatures begin to subside into 70-degree days. A cool breeze rustles the leaves in the trees, and the weather becomes temperate enough for anyone to enjoy a nature walk or an outdoor theater production. Many things can be considered hygge during the fall season, from long sweaters and luscious boots to comfortable sweatpants and delicious desserts. Not to mention the pumpkin-spiced lattes that your local coffee shop is likely to sell! Many enjoy spending time with their families, while others prefer to sit on their porch and watch the leaves slowly change colors. Many people love lighting their seasonal candles scented with autumnal spices and turning off the lights in their home, and many others enjoy lying in the dark with their windows open as the smells of the outside autumn waft in.

No matter the season, there are always opportunities for hygge. Many find their joys within the seasons, from seasonal meals and desserts to temperatures fit for bundling up or going for a walk. Sometimes it may reflect who the individual shares the season with and what the promise of a specific season means to them. Winters denote snuggling and cuddling up to those you love while watching beautiful movies, and autumn reminds people of delectable treats they will consume as they approach the holidays. Spring boasts new life and new adventures for a new year, while summer means vacation times, sun-soaked laughter, and exploration. All of this can be enjoyed with friends, family, or alone. Just remember, there is a difference between choosing to be alone and feeling lonely. The former can bring about a wonderful experience of hygge. The latter can ruin the hygge experience if it promotes sadness and negative emotions.

Again, hygge is a deep-seated feeling that transcends seasons. It wraps up those stereotypical ideas of seasons into an ongoing lifestyle. No longer are these scenes and images things to just aspire to, but the hygge philosophy can allow you to re-categorize them into a fulfilling way of life. You do not need to just dream of the next season each time you are in a season you like less. Find ways to enjoy every season, and you will discover your hygge each and every day, elevating your levels of comfort, happiness, and fulfillment.

When you fuse hygge with the seasons, it not only brings about relief and a different way of life, it also brings about hope. The hope is that the images we associate with the seasons become true-to-life experiences available to anyone, no matter what.

And sometimes, hope is all we need.

CHAPTER 6:

HYGGE ON A BUDGET

With all of the beautiful things mentioned about hygge-like moments throughout the seasons, many also need to keep things within their budget. As previously mentioned, hygge transcends social classes. Therefore, it is more than possible to implement hygge without spending a ton of money. Today's "millennials" have been proven to be the first generation that will not only make less money than their parents throughout the course of their lifetime, but they will have a lower standard of living than their parents. They will be the first generation to not progress beyond what their parents achieved, although they will establish their lifestyles differently. For example, millennials travel more, change jobs more often, and take more time off than the generations before them. And, with the high-octane culture many of these millennials live in, they will need stress relief tactics above and beyond what they are familiar with on a regular, daily basis.

The modern world's economic realities also mean today's young people need to keep hygge within a specific budget. But that is okay because you can implement hygge without spending an additional penny. Remember, turning off your phone, sitting still, and breathing is hygge. So, hygge can be free, but let's explore some of your low-cost hygge possibilities.

Many millennials cannot afford the gas money to take those luxurious mountain drives or indulge in a beachfront rental property vacation. Many more cannot afford the ingredients to cook lavish meals or purchase those $42.00 quote-inscribed candles in all their various scents. For many, merely indulging in a bath bomb is a step outside of their budget.

So, how can you create a stress-free lifestyle within the limitations of a budget?

For starters, if you are a candle lover, many websites sell off-brand candles and other candles that are not entirely up to manufacturer quality. Think of them as the "Dollar Store" of the retail world, but in candle form. You can find many rare scented candles that have inscriptions on them on websites for $5-$10, and even more websites will give discounts when you purchase a certain number of candles. Likewise, various smaller towns have legitimate candle factories, where employees create homemade candles in the back and then sell them out front. Buying candles from these types of places lowers prices drastically because they cut out the middleman. You can even purchase battery-powered electronic candles that can last far longer than a wax candle ever could. Sure, you won't get the same scent or heat emitting from them, but you will still benefit from the lighting.

When it comes to food, plenty of people do not have the budget to purchase their favorite pastry from their favorite market. But there's a way around this. Why not buy the ingredients on your own and make your own pastry? If you do not like baking, then perhaps work that pastry into your already-set grocery budget. Maybe you can dispense with that unhealthy pack of sodas or opt for cheaper toilet paper to free up some funds for your favorite pastry, all while not going over your shopping budget. Your hygge-goals have options here. Be creative!

Another way to reduce stress and find hygge-like moments that do not cost anything is to go out for a walk. Rather than getting in your car and using gas, which is detrimental to your wallet and the environment, just leave your house and stroll around your block. Consider putting headphones in but be extra careful when blocking out sounds around you—you will not hear cars in the street, people, or animals. Even if the scenery around your block isn't the most exciting, merely moving your body while listening to your all-time favorite playlist can elicit positive emotions, which have significant benefits for the overall reduction of stress as well as balancing brain chemistry. I also challenge you to find the beauty in your scenery, as beauty is everywhere. Try listing your ten favorite things about walking around your block to ensure a positive experience!

Another way to do hygge on a budget is to find a way to make your favorite coffeehouse drink. Many people spend up to $80 a month at a coffeehouse when they could spend half of that and make twice as many drinks at home. However, I understand that some people utilize their favorite coffeehouse as an excuse to get out and around people—and the experience in a coffeehouse can be hygge in itself. If that is the case, purchase small packages of your favorite flavored creamer and use them when you buy a standard coffee from your favorite coffeehouse. You'll save money in the long run and still enjoy those hygge-inducing flavors!

Another way you can do hygge on a budget is to consider creating your own entertainment. You don't need to spend money going out for a movie. There are so many streaming websites out there, although many of us do not realize just how much it costs us to have them all running. If we use too many sites, we could be racking up huge bills over the year and not really notice how much we really spend as costs of streaming from multiple sources come out of our accounts often, on different days, and in smaller bill amounts. You can also go on your computer and find entertaining videos and films on YouTube, which you do not have to pay anything for. For those looking for alternative entertainment, consider checking out your local library. You can pick out a good book, take it home, curl up on your couch, and immerse yourself in another world and it will not cost you a penny (as long as you do not bring the copy back late!). You could even get an audiobook from your library if you prefer listening to stories rather than reading them. You may even find a quiet nook in a library full of colorful nature magazines and decide that is hygge in itself. If any of this sounds like you, get yourself a library card and begin reaping the benefits of this free entertainment.

If it is too difficult to get to a library, or the cost of getting there is too expensive, you can still create hygge in your home. You can create your own nook! Dig out old blankets, find a comfy chair (or, if your budget allows, purchase a cheap bean bag chair). Stuff it with used books or anything else in your home that you consider hygge. Light the nook to perfection with candles you already have, or perhaps use a soft lamp. If you have to buy anything, perhaps scour the internet for daily deals and slowly piece something together without ever going beyond your financial means. Again, if you need to, make room in your budget by giving up something else so that you never spend beyond your means. Alternatively, you can go to thrift stores, flea markets, and rummage sales to find spectacular deals. People tend to sell used or unwanted items for a bargain—they're often trying to get rid of them more than they are trying to make a profit! Take advantage of this market to create your own nook, and before long, you can sit in your own little slice of hygge heaven.

If you decide that you need to spend a bit of money, you can find many proverbial gems at low prices. Everything from books to candleholders to antique bookshelves is sold at way below their traditional value at thrift stores. Therefore, it is easy to walk in with a small amount of cash and walk out with all the tools and items necessary to put together your dream relaxation nook. Be sure to remember mood lighting! You can use candles or twinkling fairy lights but make your space as comforting and personalized as possible, so you have the freedom to unwind. Express yourself! Paint your fantasies into it! Remember that finding hygge is all for you and all about you.

Thrift stores are not just useful for creating your own nook; you can create your own comfortable wardrobe from them. If you need new clothes and do not have money to spend on lavish items, these stores are plentiful. Many people find their most comfortable pieces of clothing hanging on the racks in thrift stores, from old knit sweaters to marked down fuzzy socks. You can find everything from handmade blankets to fleece-lined comforters, and even those who enjoy collecting coffee mugs or beer glasses will find themselves immersed in a world that their hygge thrives in. And, just like the library, many people find browsing thrift stores hygge in and of itself. Looking at all the weird and wonderful things in these stores can be enjoyable, as can trying on fun clothes you'd never opt to buy. Therefore, do not rob yourself of the joy (and incredible bargains) a thrift store might bring you. Remember, hygge is not merely about just being comfortable; it is about finding new things and ways that make you cozy. It will comfortably expand your horizons. Take advantage of that.

To benefit from another form of hygge, you could make yourself a simple, slow-cooked meal. And, before you worry about how much a chuck roast, carrots, celery, and onions cost, understand that a slow-cooked meal does not necessarily mean an expensive meal. If you purchase a package of chicken breasts and some Alfredo sauce, you can simmer that in a crockpot on low heat for six hours, boil some noodles, and have yourself an Italian feast! If Mexican cuisine is what you fancy, buy chicken breasts, dump in a jar of your favorite salsa, and cook on high for four hours. Maybe you don't like to eat meat, and you want to slow cook yourself a delicious mac 'n' cheese. Then so be it! A slow-cooked meal does not have to be expensive to make you salivate and sink into the couch while the smell wafts over you from your kitchen. A warm meal in your stomach is relaxation enough for many people, and there are several two-ingredient crockpot recipes out there that will satiate anyone. You can even cook a large amount of this meal, portion it out, and freeze whatever leftovers you have. You will then have meals for days and will therefore be able to relax in the evenings when you do not feel like cooking and cannot justify spending money on takeout.

Although a spa is relaxing to many, the cost can put it beyond a hygge budget. However, that does not mean a spa day is out of reach. Giving yourself a self-care spa day at home is simple, fun, and can be done for a relatively low price. You can purchase your favorite nail polish color and apply it yourself. Or you can use gentle hand soap and a bowl filled with warm water to soak your feet and hands in to scrub off all that dead skin. You can use bath bombs, bath salts, and skin-softening bath bubbles that will make you hum with joy. You can buy cheaper face masks, body creams, and hair masks. Better yet, you can just buy coconut oil and give your hair a deep condition. Just because you cannot afford the $300 price tag for a salon spa day doesn't mean the relaxation of a spa is out of the question! And the money you spend on a do-it-yourself spa day is a wise investment because many of the items will last longer than a single day so that you can have multiple spa days. You could incorporate these spa days into your weekly routine and have many of them. That extra bit of self-care will keep you happy and in the hygge mindset as much as possible.

It's even possible to consider therapy as hygge. We all have issues we need to discuss in one way or another. Sometimes, the best path to healing ourselves is to speak about our lives openly. Talking to a professional who offers insight when necessary may offer a more objective view of your life, which is relaxing to some. However, many therapy sessions are not covered by insurance, and many others cannot afford the insurance that does. You could then consider talking to a friend of a family member. Although talking with a friend who knows you well can prove to be even more stressful than not talking at all, it is often beneficial. If you are the more introverted type and want to benefit from a form of therapy, consider keeping a journal to externalize your thoughts. If you do not like to write with a pen, then open up a document on your laptop or desktop computer. Keep a journal (whether it's paper or electronic) to help get your thoughts out and in order. Although there might not be anyone listening, you will still be expressing your vital thoughts and emotions without judgment or ridicule. Sometimes it can be cathartic to know that your thoughts, emotions, and judgments have been unloaded somewhere and are no longer cooped up within you. Write it down, and let it go!

Also, to use a bit of self-therapy, you don't need to write diary entries or into your journal. You could write poetry, stories, or draw pictures if that's what you find relaxing and hygge-inducing. There are no right or wrong answers here, just whatever suits you best! And don't be afraid to try a combination of things. Just because you are talking with your friend about your problems doesn't mean you shouldn't also write a journal. In fact, keeping a journal will likely help you remember the issues you need to deal with and can provide a framework for you to bring up your issue with a friend in the first place.

If you are still paying for a video streaming service, then you don't need to worry about spending any additional money to find your favorite movie there. Having the steaming service and using it will always be cheaper than going to the theater, too, especially for how often you are likely to use the streaming service. Furthermore, indulging in a bit of nostalgia by watching an old film you love can conjure positive emotions that compound positivity in the body. Movies that elicit laughter and happiness cause the brain to secrete dopamine and serotonin, two of the main chemicals in the brain associated with happiness. These neurotransmitters also help preserve lifelong brain function, abate seasonal depression, and help you sleep better. So, if all you have is a streaming service, throw on a comedy or a feel-good movie that you love and get lost in it! It will leave you with more lasting effects than just making you smile in the moment.

A few people find gardening relaxing, but many people who would otherwise enjoy it are deterred by the idea of digging massive amounts of dirt while the sun is high in the sky. This is the exact reason why people invented indoor gardens. You can employ tactics from a cheap hydroponic garden all the way to potted plants that thrive without sunlight that will go easy on your pocketbook. Several people have installed kitchen sink gardens and grow anything from fresh herbs and spices all the way to their own pineapple plants from right inside their homes! Better yet, you can start many of these plants by using scraps from the foods you already purchase at the store. Simply buy the pot and soil, and you are ready to create your very own peaceful indoor garden—without the mess of a traditional garden!

Living a hygge lifestyle does not require much money. All it requires is a yearning desire to be stress-free, even if you only achieve this in spurts. Always remember that hygge is a feeling and not a concept. Concepts have rules, and sometimes those rules become expensive, like fancy diets that come with their own measuring tools. With hygge, you simply need to treat yourself kindly and remember to breathe. These two ideas side-by-side create the perfect habitat for the physical, mental, and emotional health to thrive. The hygge lifestyle lets you be creative and find activities that come at no cost to keep you relaxed throughout your day. So do not fret if you feel the pressure to spend money because that's what you think hygge is. Hygge is for everyone, everywhere, regardless of personal or financial circumstances.

You do not have to live your life in a constant state of stress-induced anxiety and exhaustion. You do not have to sacrifice yourself for your job continuously. It is possible to work hard and still find time to relax and focus on yourself.

And that is what hygge is all about: focusing on yourself.

CHAPTER 7:

HYGGE AS NEW EXPERIENCES AND CULTIVATING MEMORY

When you think of hygge, you may think of it in terms of comfort of the present moment. Although this idea is somewhat correct, hygge can also be about forming new memories by going on adventures and trying things you've always wanted to try but never given yourself the time to do so. Therefore, hygge is not exclusively about relaxing. You could find hygge in thrill-seeking moments, or in those special times that you hang out with your families. If you act in a way you know will create new, novel, and exciting memories for you, your life will be more enriched as a result. With this newfound enrichment, you will form memories that you can use as a form of hygge and comfort during your day-to-day life as you lie on your sofa, wind down after a difficult day, and retreat into nostalgia.

Although you might feel comfort in following the same routine over and over again, and you may even find this somewhat hygge in itself, you also run the risk of stagnating and becoming bored or frustrated—the antithesis of hygge. Therefore, the richness of a new experience could fulfill all your hygge needs, and the memories these experiences can form could contribute more strongly to a fulfilled life than if you were to play it safe by not stepping out from your comfort zone.

Therefore, the formation of new memories is absolutely essential to hygge. The only way you will recall old information and compare experience is through memory, and your memory will help guide you to experiences you deem to be hygge. If you cannot remember how hygge feels due to the lack of experience you've had with it, how will you draw from your knowledge in order to seek it? If you only use a lavender candle every time you wind down at the end of the day, how do you know you don't also like citrus candles? How do you know that you don't like citrus candles even more?

The answer is you won't know unless you try it. Therefore, hygge is a process of experimentation and an openness to new experiences, whether your experiences be large-scale and lifechanging like traveling to a region of the world that you've never visited before to summit a mountain, or whether the experience is as simple as adding a different flavored syrup to your morning coffee. New sensory and bodily experiences can open up a new world of hygge you may never have known you enjoyed otherwise. And perhaps you find out that you do not like something new that you tried. Fine! Then you know not to do it again. You only know what you've learned.

Psychologically, the human mind forms memories easier when it experiences significant moments. Many trivial events happen to us in our day-to-day experiences, and most of that triviality gets lost once the present moment passes. However, memories have a way of keeping a record of the past in their own unique way. Memories can be notoriously bad for recording specific details. Therefore, even if memories feel clear to an individual, there are many aspects that the brain will "imagine," filling in the gaps their memory has failed to fill itself. However, the mind tends to be good at recalling overall experiences.

Think about it. If you try to remember something that happened every hour of every day over the last week, chances are you will forget large chunks of time because nothing significant happened. However, if on your way home you tripped over your shoelace and dropped your coffee on the ground, and shared a laugh with a passerby, you'll have that in your mind and a funny story to tell at a later date. Your mind may forget exactly what you were wearing that day, omit the exact coffee you ordered, or the color of the eyes of the passerby—but you will remember the most crucial part of it clearly. If you see the funny side in this situation, you it will likely be more of a hygge-like experience when you consult your memories. Making light of otherwise embarrassing situations can lead you to feel calmer and even make you chuckle!

To apply how we form memories for hygge, consider engaging in different activities that you find new or exciting that will more likely lead to the creation of positive memories. You can also think of how we tend to do this on specific days throughout the year. People will always ask you what you did on Christmas, and the chances are you will remember because the holiday is significant. What other days is a family together, eating a delicious meal, and handing each other gifts? Not many, if any at all. Therefore, when you try to cultivate hygge in the form of a good memory, enrich your experience by testing new or novel things.

Have you always wanted to go rock climbing? Then give it a go. Not only might you enjoy the experience in itself, but you will also be able to form a positive memory that you can think back to if you keep going back and getting good at it. The same goes for cases in which you've always wanted to take up a sport, or you've always wanted to go to a national park, and you keep promising yourself you'll go, but you keep making excuses as to why you shouldn't. Once you do these things, you can determine whether you found them hygge or not. If you do, then great! You can rinse and repeat. If you do not, then no worries! You don't have to do it again. When you apply your hygge mindset to new experiences, you will increase your chances of having experiences that will lead to excellent memories that you can hold on to for the rest of your life.

Remember that, over time, memories can fade. A good way of keeping these memories alive is by writing down your experiences—which strengthens them internally and keeps a record of them externally—or taking pictures of things you do. Use these supplemental methods to assist your memory and increase your hygge experiences. Furthermore, perhaps you go on a walk every day, and you take the same route every day. Try a different route, write down how you feel about it, and maybe take some pictures of cool wildlife or a tree that makes you smile. The world around you is alive and electric. Even if you live in a city, walk down roads you have never been down before, and give your mind something new to consider. But make sure when you walk down unfamiliar streets that they are safe!

Perhaps you want to form memories, but you need to do it in the comfort of your own home. Then maybe try and do things inside that you've always wanted to do and never had the motivation to. Want to build your own shelf? Then give it a go. Want to write a letter of gratitude to a friend? Then sit and do that. When you do these things that are novel and new, not only will you enjoy them, but you will also have a new memory to show for it. And memories are fundamentally essential to us as human beings. Not only do they give us stories to share and enrich our experience when socializing with others, but they also allow us a positive sense of nostalgia when reflecting back on an exciting time in our lives. When we age, our activity levels dwindle gradually. When we have more novel memories, we can create feelings of hygge in our own heads when our bodies become less capable. Therefore, the hygge way of mixing new experiences with memories is by thinking long-term!

To truly reap the rewards of hygge memory, though, we need to ensure we have the correct perspective in everything we do. Remember that hygge is not related to material things, but to how we view the world around us and take actions based on those views.

CHAPTER 8:

HYGGE AS PERSPECTIVE

While some may experience hygge as a feeling, a philosophy, or even a fad, the fact is that hygge is a perspective. It is a way of viewing all aspects of life, from day-to-day activities to life-defining hopes and dreams. Every aspect of life will take on a hygge perspective when you begin to live a hygge lifestyle. Understanding the true nature of hygge is critical for anyone who wants to incorporate it into their way of life.

Without this understanding, hygge can go the way that countless other traditions and cultural movements such as hippies, Bohemians, and hipsters have gone: into oblivion. These traditions started as a lifestyle revolution, promoting a different approach to life, love, and happiness. They all had a direct impact for a while, affecting how people lived in a great many ways. Unfortunately, as time progressed, these movements' true nature got lost in the hype of commercialism, which replaced the hippie's outlook on life with overpriced hippie-style jeans, blouses, and even incense. Likewise, the Bohemian movement's lifestyle became little more than a fashion trend, with some musical genres incorporating the name. This cycle of events is seemingly inescapable since materialism's overwhelming influence seems to always corrupt, co-opt, and assimilate any other culture or way of life it comes into contact with. No matter how powerful a movement is when it begins, eventually, it succumbs to the relentless influences of the consumerist culture surrounding it. In other words, it goes from counterculture into mainstream culture, with the latter especially corruptible by materialism. That said, if you want to incorporate true hygge into your life, it is imperative that you keep hygge safe from the cultural assimilation that has befallen countless popular modern movements. The key is never to lose sight of the fact that hygge is a perspective and that no commercial interest or influence will ever corrupt that.

One way to keep the true nature of hygge as perspective alive and well is to continually distance the concept of hygge from the things that help manifest it. A perfect example of this is the use of candles to create a hygge environment. While it is true that candles, and the light they provide, can create a feeling of hygge in any room, referring to the candles themselves as hygge misses the point. Candles are candles, nothing more and nothing less. The experience you have with the candles could be hygge, though. Therefore, a candle branded 'hygge' would be incorrect as the material has no inherent meaning. It is your perspective that makes them hygge or not. And, as we discussed earlier, hygge comes down to your interpretation. Nothing can promise to satisfy your unique outlook on hygge.

Unfortunately, many people will begin to call candles hygge, thus starting the cycle of turning a way of life into an advertising campaign. The more we call various objects hygge, the stronger the corrupting influence will be. Such is the course of a capitalist market.

This corruption is precisely what happened to the Zen tradition. While Zen took on a unique form in Western culture—becoming something akin to hygge—it was usurped by consumerism. Now when you discuss Zen in the Western World, the first thing that another person may envision is Zen candles, Zen water fountains, or even Zen tea. In other words, rather than imagining the core feeling and mindset of Zen, many will conjure up images of the product line sold at their local market. You can undoubtedly create a Zen environment or even a Zen mindset by burning candles, listening to a water fountain, and even drinking hot tea. However, you can also create a Zen mindset by taking a walk in nature, spending time with one of your loving pets, or listening to soothing music. Sadly, the items used to achieve Zen goals have become mistaken for the goal itself. Any person who is genuinely interested in Zen and in attaining a Zen mindset will steer clear of the objects that have the name "Zen" attached to them, as they know that this is nothing more than a marketing gimmick. Buying into these products perpetuates the falsehood that Zen can be purchased in a store, and the nature of being Zen can be reduced to something that has monetary value. Fortunately, enough people are aware of the problem and are striving to return the true meaning of Zen back to its original definition. Zen, like hygge, doesn't require that you spend any more money.

But hygge faces the same challenge that Zen has faced, and still faces, in Western culture. Before long, candles will be given the moniker "hygge," as will blankets, slippers, mugs, and even varieties of hot chocolate. In fact, it will probably only be a few more Christmas seasons before you will be able to purchase a hygge gift set, complete with all of these things in a "genuine" Danish gift basket. Therefore, it is imperative that anyone who engages in the practice of hygge maintains the true meaning of the concept and upholds the individualistic, personal and anti-commercial nature of this fine tradition. Never allow yourself to buy things just because they are attributed to the hygge lifestyle—you should only buy something if it helps provide you with a genuine hygge experience. Certainly, candles help establish hygge because they allow you to turn off electric lights and unplug from modern technology. However, this doesn't mean that you need candles to be hygge, or that a candlelit room is necessarily hygge.

Let's use a metaphor. Think of hygge as getting yourself into shape. Sure, you can buy things that help you get into better shape, like weights or spinach. However, merely buying these things won't get you into better shape. You can get into shape by using them or eating them. However, you can also get into shape without buying weights or spinach. In that way, for hygge, you can buy tools or supplementary materials to help you achieve a hygge mindset, like candles. Still, candles are not absolutely essential for you to accomplish a hygge state of mind.

The most important thing is determining what hygge means to you and deciding what items are necessary to establish it in your heart and mind. After all, that is the whole point of hygge—it is the process of creating a specific state of mind. It is your perspective. It doesn't discriminate based on the seasons. This state of mind can be defined as cozy, joyful, peaceful, or any other positive word that best describes what hygge means to you. Just as hygge can mean many different things, it can also take many different things to manifest it. You should be sure not to get caught up in the 'tools of the trade.' You can find hygge despite the tools that could get you there. Keep your mind focused on the feeling of hygge and the impact that the feeling has on your life.

Another essential aspect of hygge is that it can only be understood when—and if—you consider hygge as a perspective. That aspect is that hygge comes from within, not from without. As such, the key isn't to try to find something that possesses hygge in order to create the hygge experience. Instead, the trick is to find things that *inspire* the hygge that already exists in your heart and mind.

As a state of mind, hygge is something that has to be aroused, not ingested. This state of mind is why people can find hygge in a wide array of objects and experiences. The objects and experiences don't contain hygge; instead, the individual using them possesses a hygge state of mind. Subsequently, you take hygge with you wherever you go and whatever you do. Knowing this will help keep the true meaning of hygge alive and well in your mind, and it will help you encourage others to stay on the right path towards their hygge, too!

Instead of using things traditionally associated with hygge, begin to explore all of the things that resonate with the hygge that resides within you. There will be many things that you will consider hygge—one of the most enjoyable aspects of it can be finding exactly what you determine it to be. You might be surprised at the things that can inspire a hygge response within you. They may be things associated with your childhood, or they may be things related to your favorite color, fragrance, or even flavor. Sure, hot chocolate is commonly referred to as an integral part of hygge, but if chocolate isn't your thing, it's important for you to find something else that works better. It is vital that you don't simply follow what others are doing, as this is another road to turning a lifestyle into a trendy cookie-cutter trap. Instead, use what others do as a point of inspiration. Start with hot chocolate, for example, but move on to other hot beverages that you might like, such as tea, lattes, or even hot mochas. Or you might not even like hot drinks, so you can merely try drinking orange juice instead. There is no need to latch on to the fad just for the sake of it. However, you might find that someone else uses similar tools as those you use to experience hygge. And that is fine! Even in our individual interests, there will be some overlap. Use the hygge-interests of others as inspiration for your own.

Something else to consider is the fact that hygge isn't a fixed point in time. Just because something inspires hygge one day does not mean it will have the same effect on another day. As a result, it is essential to discover various things that inspire hygge so that you can alternate among them, as your mood requires. Your perspective is absolutely crucial here. A perfect example of this is reading. For many, reading can ooze hygge. However, there might be a time when your eyes are tired, or your body isn't in the mood to sit for an extended period of time. In these cases, reading, no matter how hygge it might usually be, may not induce that feeling. Remember that you can also "read" a book using an audiobook!

Remember, hygge is flexible. Instead of reading, a walk in the woods, a bicycle ride, or any other more physical activity might suit your body's needs at that moment. Alternatively, if your eyes need a rest, then simply listening to some soothing music while you relax with your eyes closed might just do the trick. Since your mood and energy levels will change from day to day, it is vital to remain flexible with your hygge practices. By recognizing that hygge comes from within, you will depend less on specific activities to nurture your hygge state of mind. This will enable you to choose from a wide variety of things, meaning that you can access different tools to suit your different moods and energy levels.

This flexible approach to hygge can take on a seasonal connotation, especially in countries with a broader range of seasonal climates than Denmark has. In parts of the United States, where it can get extremely cold in the winter and extremely hot and sunny in the summer, tapping into different sources for hygge can be extremely beneficial. While sitting by a fire might be just do the trick in the dead of winter; relaxing on a beach, listening to the sounds of the ocean, and feeling the gentle summer breeze might do the trick in the heart of summer. Discovering your various faces of hygge will help keep you maintain a hygge state of mind all year long, regardless of the season or the weather conditions. Like everything else, the only thing that really changes is your perspective. Therefore, it is vital that you remember that your hygge is within, waiting to be "switched on," and external stimuli can help you achieve this goal. This knowledge will help keep you from getting stuck in a rut with certain hygge activities. Sure, fireplaces and hot chocolate are fantastic, but you can't rely on them in July in Florida! (And this is where the flexibility comes in—try having a delicious ice-cold drink instead.)

Therefore, by finding what inspires your hygge in every likely scenario and environment, you can rest assured that your hygge will always be within reach. Finding hygge inspiration in many things also means that you won't have to pack an extra suitcase to bring your hygge items with you when you travel. The less reliant you become on specific objects, the more likely it is that you will be able to experience hygge no matter where you are. This holds true for business trips as well as vacations. If you have to travel for business, you must find numerous and simple ways to nurture your hygge mind. It can be as simple as bringing a candle with you to the hotel, bringing a home comfort like a pillow (or even a stuffed animal!), or comfortable slippers you can wear about the room. Even business trips do not have to make hygge difficult. All you need to do is hold on to the notion that you bring your hygge with you, no matter where you go. Again, perspective is fundamental!

While it is true that you shouldn't get too caught up in specific items or activities for maintaining your hygge mind, it is also true that when you find something that works, you should use it fully. If you fall in love with a particular piece of clothing, such as a sweatshirt, and it fills you with hygge each time you wear it, then wear it as often as you can. Don't be afraid of what others might think or say. Wear your sweatshirt every day if you want, because it matters how you feel and what will give you the experience of hygge. In the case of summer clothes, maybe you have a favorite pair of sandals or a favorite t-shirt that arouses your inner hygge every time you wear it. If you want to wear socks with your sandals down to the beach, so be it! It's up to you to love what you wear, and not for other people to decide. Use it as long as it works but know that you can find other things to take its place if it stops working. Stay flexible, pay attention to your body and mind, and maximize your hygge perspective as much as possible.

Music can also affect your perspective and inspire you into hygge. Sometimes you will come across a song that just resonates completely, overflowing your hygge levels like a river in a rainstorm. You might be tempted to play the song repeatedly, listening to the music and lyrics until you feel as though you could burst with the hygge you feel. Eventually, you might wear the song out by listening to it too much, or you might find something else to take its place; however, as long as it does the job, you should listen to it as often as you can. The important thing is to keep your hygge alive and well at all times. Therefore, whenever you discover something that achieves that goal, use it as much as you possibly can, no matter how boring or annoying it might be to some people around you!

CHAPTER 9:

HYGGE AS A CREATIVE OUTLET

You can apply hygge to your creative life and use its mindset to improve how you live in various ways. Creativity can give you an abundance of mind-healing properties and meaning. Having a creative hygge mindset can enrich your experiences as you become more in tune with your inner self and your external surroundings, and you will be happier regardless of your internal or external circumstances. One of the best ways to have a healthy mind is to express yourself creatively. Just like hygge itself, creative expression manifests in various ways and can mean different things to different people. Some may find cooking an elaborate meal or baking a delicious homemade treat to be a profoundly creative act. Some may find hygge in the more traditional artistic outputs—painting, sewing, writing poetry, singing, taking pictures and editing them, making homemade videos, and even dream journaling. You may even find it creative to make that nook in your house that we discussed earlier!

One of the main benefits you can get from engaging in a creative activity to foster a hygge state of mind is that you can use your individuality to express yourself in an authentic and calming way. You can express the strength of who you are most effectively if you apply the principles of hygge to every "brushstroke" of your creative efforts.

You can find comfort even from your darkest thoughts if they manifest tangibly in front of you, no matter whether you are writing or taking photographs. Perhaps you've always wanted to take up a creative hobby and, up until now, you've made an excuse for yourself like "I'm always too busy" or "I'm always too tired." Well, when you apply hygge, you will find more energy. You can make creativity a habit and use it to foster hygge.

There's a difference between the traditional work-oriented mindset plaguing those who live in the US and that of other Western societies. Often, an American feels too busy to engage in what they perceive as "play." They usually center their focus around their work and jobs, to the detriment of meaningful creative expression.

Creativity is fundamental to a healthy mind. Although it can be playful, it goes well beyond this narrow definition (in a way similar to the fact that hygge goes well beyond mere comfort). Therefore, in order to foster a hygge mindset creatively, it is essential to free up some time on your calendar and start using your mind and body to create something special and meaningful for you. It is in this freeing up and boundless potential for creativity that makes hygge possible for any individual.

To direct your energy onto something creative will help you maximize your enjoyment of life and potentially provide you with an abundance of hygge. Creativity can be relaxing, help alleviate stress, and help individuals make peace with their environment. Too often, we can feel stuck indoors and bored with nothing to do. We scroll endlessly through newsfeeds on our phones, and buy things we don't need to try and fill the meaning-shaped hole burning inside us. There may be days that you want social interaction, but all of your friends and family are busy. Therefore, there's nothing quite like creating art and indulging yourself in these quieter moments of solitude and self-reflection.

Your options for what you consider hygge are endless. You can make art, enjoy it yourself, or take pictures of it and share it with your friends and family. Hey, it might even be hygge for you to write a poem or paint a piece of art, and then let it go by throwing it on a fire—whatever is most hygge for you! If you share it with friends and family, and they, too, are dedicated to the hygge mindset, they may even take up a creative activity themselves. This attitude will provide you with a chance to explore yourself individually when it comes to a creative expression of hygge and spread the good vibes to others around you!

Have you ever walked around an art gallery, read an incredible book, or watched a brilliant film, and wished you could create something beautiful yourself? The best news is that you can, even if you've never engaged in the hobby before. Look at any actor, poet, artist, or singer. They all had to start somewhere, and when they began to express themselves, it wasn't the fantastic stuff we all get to experience today. We all have to start somewhere and accept that we are the well-to-do fool on the quest for mastery. In short: there's no shame in being a beginner.

The sheer act of creation comes with a multitude of benefits. By writing stories or journaling, we can make sense of our lives through narrative, as humans are naturally narrative driven. We can laugh, cry, release, and express through this form of creativity uniquely. It is a way to externalize our minds even if there is not a single person around to experience it with us. But if there are other people around, we can share our stories with others. Consider how great it is when others share stories with you.

Consider how much you love telling stories yourself. They are a way for us to bond and come together over the dinner table with family or in a café sipping coffee with a friend.

If you're too self-conscious about your artistic output or feel low on energy, you can engage in less taxing forms of self-expression. For example, you could start a collage. Take magazines you love, images off the internet, or words and phrases from a newspaper you have. Cut them up and stick them on a board that best reflects what hygge means to you. You can find positive words from the newspaper and pictures of people smiling in the sun or the snow. It all depends on what fosters hygge within you. Perhaps hygge means a variety of things to you that are distinct from one another. Maybe you love summer and winter equally. Perhaps you could create two different collages, one for summer and one for winter. Or maybe you could do a collage where you dedicate half of it to winter and the other half of it to summer. The contrast could even be beautifully hygge itself! You could incorporate your own thoughts and feelings in the collage by creatively cutting out words from various headlines and making them say what you want them to say.

You could even engage in the creative process with the word "hygge" specifically in your mind, or you could even write it on a sticky note and put it in front of you as a constant reminder to your conscious and subconscious mind. Perhaps you can write a poem that features the word hygge. You could make rhymes about precisely what it means to you and the positive impact it could potentially have in your world. Before you get creative, you could even make your favorite drink, have a glass of wine, or eat a square of dark chocolate—whatever is most hygge for you! You could sit in the nook you may have already made in your home, or you could go out into nature and draw under a tree, or sit and write a poem in your favorite café. The possibilities really are endless.

To think about the present mindedness that poetry can bring to the hygge mindset, envision the Japanese poetry of haiku. Haiku is a three-line poem under 17 syllables. It often reflects one moment in nature and captures it in the form of a written snapshot. Haiku writers will look at the natural world and convert it into a satisfying moment of beauty, seeing simplicity (although, if you ask a haikuist, you will realize how complicated it really is). Haiku helps the mind be more hygge. It encourages the writer to interpret the natural world more regularly and pay attention to the present moment rather than rushing around to do the next thing on the never-ending to-do list.

If you decide to do something like writing a story or a poem, or you start taking stunning pictures and editing them, you can share them with others. Perhaps in your city, there are poetry open mic nights. Perhaps there are local galleries you could share your photos in. You could even hang pictures you make and poems you write in your home to remind you of hygge at all possible moments in the day.

If you're an extrovert, you could even have social art sessions. You could all sit with friends and do a writing prompt and share the results with each other after, or you could sit with your friends, sip delicious wine, and focus on creating art. You can even regress back to the days of childhood and finger paint! Anything that encourages a hygge state of mind works here.

If you are struggling and unsure of what to do about creativity, perhaps you can start a dream journal. A dream journal is basically as it sounds—a journal where you log your dreams. As soon as you wake up, record your dreams in the present tense, as if the dream were happening right in front of you. Doing this is essential for a variety of reasons. First, you will recall your dreams more easily and see connecting themes throughout different dreams you have. The positive aspect to this is that your dreams' healing capabilities will improve and your subconscious interaction with your conscious brain will be more robust. Having the subconscious and the conscious brain work symbiotically can lead to greater satisfaction, let you focus your energy where you really need to in life, and will help you develop a balanced hygge state of mind.

The problem with some of Western society and why so many of us are unhappy is that we are a consumerist culture rather than a culture of creation. If we spent less time-consuming other people's work, and more time producing our own, we would benefit from a hygge state of mind more often, and we would be more satisfied. If you're lucky and fully creatively engaged and motivated by that energetic spark, perhaps you could even experience a "flow-state" as a result of your creative expression. This state, coined by psychologist Mihaly Csikszentmihalyi, a cofounder of positive psychology, is "The best moments (that) usually occur if a person's body or mind is stretched to its limits in a voluntary effort to accomplish something difficult and worthwhile." Therefore, if you engage in a creative practice, you are placing a necessary demand for your intellectual faculties. Although hygge is about a state of pleasure and relaxation, you can experience both of these when expressing yourself with a paintbrush, pen, or camera.

The most important way to merge hygge and creativity is to realize the stress-relieving and happiness-inducing effects of it. Externalizing what goes on in your brain is exceptionally hygge as it leads to an overall sense of wellbeing. When you sit down to be creative, perhaps put on your favorite music, or even just the sounds of a waterfall or chirping birds to get you into that mindset. Make the area you are creative in as comfortable and hygge-like as possible. Perhaps put blankets and pillows on the floor before you start writing something, throw on some sweatpants instead of those uncomfortable jeans, light some candles, or use an aromatic diffuser to delight your senses as you delve deep into your inner self.

Creativity and hygge go hand in hand. You can decorate your house, paint, write, take pictures, sing, and find so many ways to express yourself. There's a reason why so many people choose to express themselves even though the process can sometimes be a little complicated. We may even hit creative "block," which is better to think of as a creative "hurdle"—a challenge to jump over, not be stopped by. Indulge in the marriage between your conscious and subconscious mind and take up a hygge-like creative endeavor whenever the feeling and mood suits you!

And with that, we can move into what hygge can do for you more broadly and how you can apply it to all aspects of your day-to-day life.

CHAPTER 10:

HOW TO BRING HYGGE INTO EVERYTHING

t's easy to find advice and tips on discovering or creating an environment that provides and nurtures a strong sense of hygge. From turning a cozy corner in a room into a hygge shrine or nook to locating that perfect place in nature that oozes hygge, establishing a space for all your hygge needs is essential. Some will call this space their "happy place." Others will just call it relaxing. Whatever you decide to call it, the point is that you should feel hygge in everything that you do. Once you realize that hygge is a perspective, you will understand that you can find it in just about any environment. While I highly recommend creating a sacred space or finding a perfect sanctuary in order to restore your hygge, it is not the only way to practice hygge in your day-to-day life. Instead, the trick is to practice hygge in even the unlikeliest of places. When you are able to restore and nurture your hygge no matter where you are, and no matter what you are doing, you will be well on your way to creating and benefitting from the hygge lifestyle. Implementing hygge no matter the situation is a critical difference between someone who dabbles in hygge and someone who adopts hygge as their way of life. The art of practicing hygge anywhere and at any time might be difficult at first, but once you get the hang of it, it will soon become second nature to you. And it is because of this second nature that you will genuinely benefit from all that hygge has to offer.

Some of the environments where you can practice hygge might not be ones you would expect to find on a list of recommendations. That is because a lot of times, when you think or read about hygge, you encounter hygge stereotypes. Therefore, it's best to look at examples of where you can practice hygge and get the most out of your new lifestyle and mindset. One such example is the grocery store. Depending on your personality, going to the grocery store might be a fun thing to do, or it might fill you to the core with dread. From having to deal with crowds of people to spending more money than you ever wanted to, grocery shopping can be a challenge even for the most easygoing people. How you react to this experience can determine how well you cope with the stress of it. Herein lies the true nature of hygge. Rather than wishing yourself away from the moment, longing to be in your quiet and cozy home far away from the hustle and bustle, utilize some of the hygge techniques you've been learning in this book into your grocery shopping experience. How you do this is up to you, but one option is to bring some earbuds and play some hygge music to drown out the stressful environment around you. Another trick is to treat yourself to something that restores your hygge state of mind. Fortunately, many grocery stores have incorporated coffee shops, making this practice easier than it would have been not so long ago. Rather than running through the grocery store at full speed in order to get out as soon as possible, take a moment to buy a cup of coffee, maybe even a pastry, and casually roam through the aisles as you indulge in something that brings you to a state of hygge. By taking things easier, you can get your grocery shopping done without stressing yourself out in the process. Furthermore, by establishing this routine, you will stop dreading your visits to the grocery store. In fact, you might even start looking forward to them, and appreciate the hygge benefits they can offer!

Another example of turning an unpleasant situation into a hygge experience is when you are stuck in traffic. Driving back and forth to work every day can be stressful enough without any added hassles. Unfortunately, those added hassles will too often find their way into your commute. Sitting in traffic and hearing the proverbial clock tick second by second can be enough to drive anybody crazy—especially if you're already late.

The thing about scenarios like these is that they are beyond our control. Not only are they unpredictable, but they are also utterly unchangeable once you find yourself in them. Rather than letting such circumstances create untold levels of stress and anxiety, take the opportunity to restore your hygge with the added time you suddenly have. One way to make sitting in traffic better is to play some music that helps to restore your spirits. If you run the risk of being stuck in traffic from time to time, make sure that you have special CDs, music tapes, playlists, or even books on tape specifically designed for those occasions. By creating a playlist to get you through that situation, you can turn any traffic delay into a hygge experience, thereby restoring your energies and relieving stress. You can even decide to do a bit of learning by listening to an audiobook or a podcast. Heck, you could try and do a guided breathing meditation as you slowly move through traffic. Doing so will lower your heart rate and cortisol, making your trip relaxing, enjoyable, and hygge. Now, instead of getting to your destination tired and frustrated, you can arrive rested with a smile on your face and a skip in your step. Engaging in activities like the listed examples will ensure that circumstances do not determine your mood, and this will help cultivate your hygge mindset at all times.

The workplace is yet another environment that can cause all sorts of stress and anxiety if you do not treat it with the all-important hygge mindset. This is especially true for anyone who works in an office setting where the décor is drab and boring at best and downright depressing and claustrophobic at worst. Cubicles, gray carpets, beige walls, and fluorescent lights can drain the energy from anyone, no matter how cheerful their disposition might be. The trick is to make sure that you have the opportunity to unplug from the dull, drab surroundings and immerse yourself in some healthy hygge energy. Pictures and objects that inspire hygge can go a long way in turning any lifeless workplace into a hygge environment. Unfortunately, not everyone has the option of decorating their workplace. Therefore, they need to employ other methods of maintaining hygge at work. One alternative method is to make use of aromatherapy. While you might not be able to burn incense or light a candle, you can still utilize fragrant scents in order to evoke a strong sense of hygge. Placing a dab of essential oil just over your upper lip will enable you to breathe your favorite fragrance all day long, with the added benefit of not bothering anyone else. You can keep several different bottles of oil on your desk or in your drawer so that you can keep the scent strong all day long. Additionally, you can change scents during the day to suit your mood. Just be sure to use essential oils that are gentle on the skin and that can wash off easily with just warm water.

You can also try things like bringing hand creams and lip balms with you to work. That way, you can take care of your skin while you sit at your desk, increasing the amount of hygge you're likely to feel at work. Keeping your skin healthy will keep you relaxed and help get you through the day in the calmest and best mood possible for the circumstances!

As mentioned earlier, music can go a long way to establishing a positive hygge mood. Some workplaces will allow you to listen to music as you work, in which case you can create your hygge environment quite easily on a regular basis. However, in the case that you cannot listen to music while you work, make sure that you bring some tunes with you anyway because you can plug your favorite music in while you eat lunch or take a coffee break. This can make all the difference in the world, helping to transport you to your happy place, thereby restoring your mind to a full sense of hygge before tackling the rest of the workday.

When you combine the use of music with the use of essential oils, you will engage two of your five physical senses, meaning that nearly half of your senses will be devoted to creating and maintaining a hygge state of mind. If you can also have visual aids, such as pictures or objects on your desk or screen savers, you can take time to focus three of your five senses on achieving hygge. When you can devote most of your physical senses to hygge, you will achieve more substantial results in no time.

Another thing you can do while you're at work is to use your lunch break to do something that's more hygge-oriented. If you bring your own lunch to work, then you don't need to worry about getting out and finding lunch, which will save you both time and money. Perhaps, then, you can go for a walk outside and sit on a bench and eat your lunch in nature. Or maybe it's too cold outside, but your office has long hallways.

Then maybe you could do a bit of exercise to keep your mind alive. You can walk the hallways as mentioned above, or even the stairs, to get in a little bit of exercise. Not only will this keep you healthier, but it will recharge your brain by flooding it with natural and healthy chemicals so you'll be ready to tackle the second half of your workday.

The effect of using objects to achieve a hygge mindset should not be underestimated. In fact, the use of objects to induce a chosen state of mind is practiced worldwide in many different forms. A prime example of using objects is in the context of religion. Millions of people worldwide, including religious people, use objects and symbols daily to evoke a sacred mindset or remind them of their particular faith. These objects can come in many different shapes and sizes. Sometimes they will be large and prominent whereas other times they will be small and discrete. No matter the event or circumstance, the impact that these objects can have is often beyond measure. Fortunately, the very same dynamic can be achieved with regard to hygge. The fact of the matter is that particular objects and symbols can evoke a strong sense of hygge within a person, much like a cross or a Buddha-figure can evoke spiritual feelings within a Christian or Buddhist, respectively. That said, it is absolutely critical that you discover what objects or symbols have this effect on you. As mentioned earlier, placing objects on your desk at work can profoundly impact your creation of a hygge environment at your workplace. However, when that option isn't available, you can try to incorporate smaller objects, such as jewelry, to achieve the same goal. You can pick something sentimental to you or something that makes you feel more positive and puts you in a go-getter mood. You could even wear a locket that has a picture of loved ones inside it. There's no right or wrong choice here. It only matters that whatever you choose inspires hygge in you!

When you wear a bracelet, ring, or even a watch that holds a particular hygge significance, you can evoke a hygge mindset each time you look at it. The trick is to find several such accessories or pieces of jewelry that have a hygge feel to them so that you can surround yourself with them as often as possible. Additionally, having numerous pieces of hygge jewelry or accessories will mean you have a hygge object to accompany formal wear, casual wear, and everything in between. The benefit, then, is that you can be hygge no matter what type of clothing the day calls for. Again, keep in mind that hygge means something different to different people. Therefore, the trick is to find what objects create a sense of hygge for you. Cat charms, pendants, or earrings can have this effect, especially if they remind you of being at home in your cozy chair with your cat in your lap. Alternatively, natural stone bracelets or pendants might remind you of your favorite place in nature, which can also evoke a hygge mindset. You might wear a watch or a piece of jewelry from your favorite museum or another place you go that helps you restore your spirit after spending time in the bustling world and restore your hygge energy.

Clothing is also a potentially powerful tool for creating hygge energy. As mentioned previously, certain comfortable clothes can help establish a sense of hygge when you are at home. However, you might not want to opt for these clothes outside of the home—and you may be completely unable to wear them if you are at work. No matter how hygge they can feel, you just can't show up to work in your favorite pajamas! But just because you can't wear your comfortable pants or sweatshirt to work doesn't mean you can't find clothes that inspire hygge. In addition to comfort, color is another way that clothes can foster hygge. Different colors inspire different moods in people, so it is vital that you take the time to find out which colors inspire a sense of hygge in you. Colors associated with winter might remind you of cozy environments, which could create a hygge mindset whenever you wear them. Or you might choose earth tones to remind you of your favorite nature retreat. The mere act of wearing your favorite color might help you complete that task at work, and you might even sense a glow from your coworkers. Maybe the clothing you wear will even inspire a feeling of hygge in them. In the end, no particular color is necessarily hygge in and of itself. Instead, a particular color should represent a hygge place or a hygge experience in you. Take the time to find colors that restore your hygge energy and make sure to fill your closet with them. This awareness and action will enable you to bring a little hygge with you everywhere you go.

So, our day-to-day actions and choices can affect our experience of hygge. It doesn't matter where you are, what you're going to do, or what type of clothing you need to wear, hygge truly can be brought into everything. You can bring it to your home, workplace, car, school, family gatherings, park, bar, theater, and anywhere else you might go. The essential lesson from hygge is that you can enjoy pretty much anything if you bring a hygge mindset to it. Whenever you next feel stressed, or you're dreading going into work or getting in that car, just remind yourself that you always have hygge. Once you recognize that you have it with you at all times, your life will improve drastically.

Now that you've learned how to bring hygge into everything, let's move forward and see how hygge manifests itself in Western culture.

CHAPTER 11:

SIGNS OF HYGGE IN WESTERN CULTURE

Although hygge is a Scandinavian word that cannot be easily translated into English, it does not mean the concept itself is alien to Westerners. Just because the English language does not have a single word that epitomizes the idea of hygge does not mean that it is not prevalent throughout Western culture. However, when you begin to truly understand the concept of hygge—which you are well on your way to doing so as a result of how much of this book you have already read—you will realize that these seemingly isolated phenomena are actually different elements of hygge emerging within Western culture. That said, it's no wonder that so many people are becoming interested in a hygge-like philosophy, no matter what they are calling it, as the seeds for it have already begun to take root under different names. Once you connect the dots of these different forms, you will begin to get a clearer idea of the essence of hygge from a Western perspective. It is not critically important that a single word cannot encapsulate hygge. What is essential is that the spirit of hygge is fully understood. Only then can hygge be implemented to its full potential within the life of an individual and within Western society as a whole.

One of the earliest forms of hygge that's prevalent in Western culture is tea consumption in England. For the past couple of centuries, drinking tea has been the cure-all for almost any trauma or circumstance imaginable. Just as a cup of coffee has become necessary for many to start the day in the USA, the proverbial English "cuppa" has become the go-to for dealing with any stressful situation. Tea-drinking is a perfect example of hygge in Western culture. In order to fully appreciate the similarities, it is essential to understand better how drinking tea becomes a part of someone's life in England and much of Great Britain. Initially, a person is introduced to tea at a young age, usually drinking a milky version of the beverage prepared and served by their mother (due to its caffeine content). This can sometimes evolve into the "tea party" game in which a child pretends to serve tea to their guests, usually comprised of several stuffed animals of various shapes and sizes. Tea drinking is a ritual of comfort and is used on any occasion. And this is where drinking tea begins to acquire its hygge status. After all, the mere act of drinking tea could become enough to take a person back to the innocent and safe days of their childhood. Just a sip could conjure up memories of a mother or father brewing them some delicious tea. Even if not, when an English person goes to someone else's house, one of the first things they will likely be offered is a cup of this hot beverage. It's no wonder that tea is the first thing that many people go for when trying to cope with a stressful situation. Nothing else can restore a sense of comfort and safety for a British person quite like a good cup of tea.

Perhaps the example of tea explains why the word "cozy"—although it goes part of the way in explaining hygge—does not fully capture hygge. If an English person had to choose a single word to describe the feeling that a cup of tea provides, cozy will likely not be at the top of the list. However, it is still an act of hygge! But words like "homey," "safe," "peaceful," and even "comfort" might come to mind, but even then, no two people will necessarily agree on which word works best, as we all should know by now. The fact is that a cup of tea evokes feelings that no single word can express fully, but there's an emotion there all the same.

Furthermore, a cup of tea can evoke different feelings in different people. Therefore, rather than trying to find that single word that expresses the true meaning of hygge, we should stick to finding examples of hygge that Westerners are already familiar with. Thus, when trying to describe hygge to someone in England, you can say that it is like drinking a cup of tea, and they will instantly understand the essence of hygge, which, after all, is far more important than the word itself.

Another form of hygge that can already be found in Western culture is the concept of "comfort food." In essence, this concept follows the tradition of hygge in two ways. First, it reflects the use of the term hygge as a root word, forming words already discussed, such as hyggebukser (hygge-pants), hyggelig (hygge-like), and hyggekrog (hygge-corner). In this way, the term 'comfort food' serves the very same function. The second way that comfort food reflects the tradition of hygge is comfort foods are particular to an individual, so not everyone will find comfort in the same foods. While these foods can differ from person to person, certain common denominators keep the various choices within the same category. One such common denominator is the simplicity of the food itself. Comfort food often includes pizza, pasta, or a bag of chips with dip—all things that are easy to make and equally easy to eat. They also tend to be hearty and unhealthy. Therefore, comfort foods aren't usually foods you can indulge in each and every day.

Again, if you were to ask for a single word to describe the feeling that eating pasta evokes, you would get many different answers. Some might say that it feels "homey," especially if they grew up in a home where their parents made pasta often. Others might say it feels "cozy" due to the warmth of the food. While all of these descriptions may be true, they aren't necessarily interchangeable. The inability to find a single word to express the feeling that a bowl of pasta creates comes from the same problem of trying to find one word that expresses the essence of hygge—it means something different for each and every person. Also, every person treats their pasta differently. Some will put salt and chili flakes on theirs. Some will put a mountain of cheese on it, whereas others will use little or no cheese. The experience of eating pasta has choices much like hygge does. No matter how you may eat your pasta, the complexity of the emotion experienced makes it challenging to define in a single word, much like the tea example used earlier in this chapter. That said, the word "comfort" is perhaps one word that can be used to define the essence of hygge. However, rather than searching for that elusive word, it might be best to say that hygge is like eating a bowl of pasta, making perfect sense to anyone who feels in their heart and mind that pasta is a comfort food.

Herein lies another way in which comfort food is a perfect example of hygge. While pasta might be comfort food for some, it may not make the list for others. Instead, they may see things like chips as comfort food. What makes a particular thing a comfort food isn't the food itself. Instead, it is the feeling that the food evokes in the individual. It is up to the individual to find out which foods create the desired result. For some, it may be warm foods such as oatmeal, pancakes, or the like. For others, it might be foods like cheese and crackers or popcorn. The fact that popcorn is fun to make can make it a perfect candidate for comfort food. When you make it in the pan, you get to watch and hear the "pop" of your ensuing snack. Popcorn can evoke true indulgence. You can put salt on it, sugar, cheese—anything that makes it comforting. It can also be paired with your favorite movie and evoke the nostalgia of going to the cinema with family. And maybe you don't even enjoy popcorn, and that's okay. It means there's more for the rest of us!

Perhaps the most outstanding example of hygge that has shifted into Western society's popular consciousness is one that has faced a similar linguistic challenge as hygge—the concept of Zen. What the term "Zen" has come to mean in Western culture is something completely different from what it means in its original East Asian cultural context. In the East, Zen is nothing more than a person's seated position when they are meditating. The word itself is an abbreviation of the word 'Zazen.' In essence, you can think of the term Zen as another word for "cross-legged." With this in mind, you begin to see how the term has come to mean something altogether different in the West than it does in the East. After all, how can you have a "cross-legged" mindset? How can the fragrance of a candle be considered "cross-legged"? Yet in the West, we use "Zen" to describe mindsets, atmospheres, responses to stress, and yes, even candle scents. This is because the lifestyle of those who practiced Zen meditation became something that Westerners began to crave, specifically the idea of transcending stress, negativity, and fear—things that are all too common in Western society. Thus, the term Zen was then used as a single word description for the results of meditation, not the meditation itself. Now the term has taken on such nebulous meaning that most people are wholly unaware of its origins.

Another aspect of Western Zen that reflects hygge is its focus on simplicity. Enjoying a walk through the woods or across the beach is considered Zen. Not only does it help a person reconnect with nature, but it can also lead to a state of peace and happiness without the need to use or purchase objects. Merely being content with what you have is a fundamental premise of Western Zen, and this ideal is also an integral part of the hygge culture too. More and more people are becoming aware of the fact that materialism doesn't bring the happiness that the societies we live in promise. Instead, materialism creates an insatiable hunger for acquiring more and is self-reinforcing. While each possession may provide happiness for a while, that happiness is fleeting, giving way to the desire to acquire yet more objects to provide that quick-fix of fleeting happiness. It's like a dog chasing its own tail on a societal level. Doing away with boundless materialism is where Zen can be most useful. Instead of finding pleasure in acquiring objects, Zen focuses on finding pleasure in the simple things in life. Again, these things' exact nature differs from person to person, just as it does in hygge. The important thing is that each individual finds those simple things that can bring them real and lasting happiness, and this "thing" will likely extend beyond getting the newest something-or-other.

In many ways, Zen's Western concept isn't altogether that much different from the concept of hygge. A Zen place is a place of peace and tranquility. Likewise, a Zen mindset is a frame of mind accepting events and circumstances that allow for serenity and calm. When a person has a Zen attitude, they don't allow themselves to be affected by criticism, anger, or other negative emotions, either from others or within. While these things may not seem to reflect the "cozy" nature of hygge, they do represent the aim of hygge, which is to restore peace and equilibrium to the heart and mind of the individual. Thus, the two concepts are closely related, even though they are different manifestations of the same principle. What makes this so essential is the fact that Zen has become such an influential part of Western culture, even though it is an entirely different entity from the original concept of Zazen. The Western tradition of Zen as the desire to achieve inner peace and harmony reflects a desire to abandon the fast-paced, cutthroat competitive paradigm of Western society. This same desire creates fertile ground in the West for hygge to take root and thrive.

The fact that the word "Zen" is used to describe a variety of different things demonstrates that no other single word can achieve that goal. There simply isn't a word in the English language that can adequately define the feeling or the experience of Zen. Rather than striving to find a replacement word, Zen merely got adopted as a term and acquired new definitions and purposes. While some might see this as sacrilege against Zen's original concept, the fact is that it represents a need within Western culture for something lacking.

That is, until now. The culture of hygge is in many ways equivalent to the Western idea of Zen, albeit without the same spiritual connotations. While yoga and meditation aren't necessarily required for hygge, they can certainly help inspire it. Thus, rather than trying to find alternate words to describe hygge and what it means, it probably would be best for Western society to simply adopt the word much the way it adopted the word 'Zen.' Then, instead of trying to explain hygge, people can simply recognize the hygge concepts they are already familiar with and begin to incorporate them into their lives in a more meaningful way. And with that, we can fully explore what hygge can do for an individual.

CHAPTER 12:

THE IMPACT OF HYGGE ON THE INDIVIDUAL

When a person develops a hygge lifestyle, they will discover many benefits manifesting in their life. We addressed some of these benefits in previous chapters, such as a marked decrease in stress and anxiety, which profoundly impacts a person's physical and mental well-being. However, there are additional benefits that will have just as profound an impact on a person's day-to-day life as the result of living a lifestyle in tune with hygge principles. Some of these benefits are a direct consequence of hygge, whereas others are more of an indirect consequence due to the changes made by hygge living. Whether direct or indirect, the one thing that all of these benefits have in common is that they are monumentally positive. This means that hygge is more than a feel-good practice. Hygge is a way of improving your life in a meaningful and results-driven way. The fact is that hygge can bring about positive changes in physical health, mental health, general well-being, relationships, performance at work, and even financial stability. In the end, when you ensure that hygge is second nature, all other aspects of your life will fall into place, which will provide you with the stability and freedom that few other lifestyles can offer.

The fact that hygge can improve a person's physical and mental health and well-being is relatively obvious to anyone who implements the hygge lifestyle. However, because it can also help improve a person's financial well-being is less obvious. Yet, this is a genuine and significant part of the impact that hygge can have on an individual. An easy way to portray the financial impact of hygge is to draw a comparison between hygge and another Western tradition that has hygge-like qualities—minimalism. The tradition of minimalism is similar to hygge in that it focuses on a person's quality of life in terms of experience rather than possessions. Doing away with needless possessions, which are often seen as "objects of attachment" by minimalists, is one of the goals of minimalism. As discussed, one of the defining aspects of modern Western culture is materialism. This manifests in the hyper-consumerist nature of industrialized societies. Unfortunately, the joy and lasting happiness that are promised once material goods are purchased perish after some short-term gratification. In other words, the end result is a brief high, followed by a crash, much like what you would experience if you ate a piece of cake for lunch. Just as you would be left hungry after a brief energy buzz and require more sustaining food for after you ate the cake, you too are left hungry for more products once the high has worn off from your last purchase.

Minimalism, like the hygge lifestyle, recognizes that this vicious cycle is not only self-defeating, but it is also extremely dangerous. After all, it is the constant craving for that temporary high that leads millions of people into crushing levels of debt year after year, something which minimalism can help alleviate.

In an attempt to free people from the consumerist mindset, minimalism encourages people to find joy in everyday activities. Again, minimalists work to shift the focus away from the unbounded promises delivered by capitalism. When a person is able to find happiness in simple pleasures, they no longer need to purchase objects to satiate their craving for fulfillment. Instead, they can maintain happiness in a very real and lasting way, just as a person can maintain energy levels by eating healthier foods. This breaks the addictive cycle of hyper-consumerism, thereby improving a person's overall state of well-being. Since the hygge mindset focuses on enjoying life's simple pleasures, just like minimalism, it offers many of the same benefits. With hygge, you will realize that life is measured in the number and quality of experiences you have, not the number of things you own.

Replacing one's focus or dependence on consumer goods is where hygge can positively impact a person's financial well-being. Every year, we all spend money on goods that we don't need. We continuously buy these things because we are promised a great deal of happiness if we purchase a particular product. Unfortunately, this promise usually falls short, resulting in another purchase to experience the same fleeting high. However, we can break this seemingly endless cycle by following the hygge tradition. By finding happiness in life's simple pleasures through hygge techniques, people can free themselves from constantly spending money when they don't need to. Once you start finding happiness in the things you already have and in the places you already go, you will no longer need to keep spending more money to be happy. Not only will this happiness be more satisfying and long-lasting, but it will also keep you from going into debt as a result of buying product after product, chasing after the empty promises pushed by creative advertising campaigns. Therefore, when you begin to follow a hygge lifestyle, you will be able to save a considerable amount of money and use that money to bring better experiences into your life, thereby improving your life in a way that you most likely would not have expected otherwise.

Another way that hygge can significantly improve a person's life is in terms of personal relationships. All too often, people find themselves wishing that they could spend time with friends and family, if only they had more time available. This is the problem with continually focusing on work instead of the things that make up the rest of a person's life. One thing that hygge promotes is a change of priorities. When you begin to practice hygge, you will start to spend less time running the proverbial 'rat race' and more time on the things that truly matter. Once you slow down, you will free up valuable time that you can then spend with the special people in your life. You will no longer have to lose touch with the people close to your heart. Needless to say, this will improve your relationships by giving them much-needed attention. The problem with neglected relationships is that no matter how much people may mean to you, the relationship can become stale. This can result in feelings of estrangement and isolation, which can not only ruin a relationship, but can also have devastating effects on your emotional health and well-being.

Herein lies another considerable benefit that hygge can provide—an improved state of mental and emotional well-being. When people become estranged from family and friends due to not having enough time to spend together, they can begin to feel isolated and alone. The more a person feels isolated and alone, the bigger life's problems can become to them. When you can talk to other people about day-to-day issues, you can face those issues with greater confidence. Not only are you able to get the stress and anxiety off your chest, but by talking things over, you might also be able to get advice and insight that can help you solve your dilemmas. Of course, this isn't a direct aspect of hygge, in the sense that the hygge lifestyle isn't about solving life's problems. However, by spending more time with other people, you can avoid the feeling of having to face life alone, and this can make all the difference in the world. When you have friends and family close by, and you foster positive and enriched experiences with these people, you will never feel alone. The emotional support that their presence alone provides can be invaluable in terms of being able to cope with difficult events. Thus, the togetherness that hygge promotes can have significant and authentic effects on stress reduction and emotional stability. These values are vital for surviving the fast-paced culture of Western society. Plus, you might find spending time with loved ones to be hygge in and of itself, so you can achieve goals you set out for your hygge lifestyle by being close to those that matter.

Another indirect benefit of hygge is that it can actually improve your performance at work. This may seem like a bit of a stretch at first, but hygge has the potential to improve every single facet of a person's life. Remember, in a previous chapter, we discussed how you could make your workplace more hygge? Well, implementing hygge can increase your performance at work, and the reason for it is quite simple. When you practice hygge in your day-to-day life, you will begin to reduce your general anxiety levels. Since stress and anxiety undermine your ability to perform to your full potential—at work and in other areas of life—and you reduce these by implementing hygge, your performance levels will increase.

Furthermore, by reducing your general levels of stress and anxiety, you will find that you can deal with day-to-day stresses at work more effectively. When your mindset is calm and more relaxed to start with, challenging days at work won't be as stressful as they were before. Therefore, by practicing hygge day to day, you can put yourself in a healthier and stronger frame of mind that will enable you to handle your work more effectively. When you handle work more effectively, you will likely come home in a better mood. Ensuring that you implement hygge at work not only affects who you are and how you feel at work but also all other aspects of your life. Work-life, home life, family life, and everything else are symbiotic. Never forget this.

Remember that it's a myth that hygge can only be experienced in specific environments; we do not need to fall prey to Western society's desire to compartmentalize things. Hygge doesn't require a particular home or outdoor environment; it is all dependent on the mindset. You can maintain that mindset wherever you are, no matter what you're doing, and regardless of the 'things' around you.

A perfect example of this truth can be found in a standard laundromat in Copenhagen. If you go to a laundromat in the U.S., you might be lucky enough to find a TV, or maybe a video game or two. However, this is far from guaranteed. Alternatively, in Copenhagen, you can find laundromats that have cafes. Now, rather than dividing your time up in terms of chores and time for yourself, you can combine the two. While doing laundry is a chore, it doesn't have to be a dreaded chore. Instead, people in Copenhagen sip hot drinks and eat delicious food while their clothes are spun clean. Anyone would be happy to do laundry with laundromats like that! And that's the point. Hygge isn't about escaping the mundane or obligatory aspects of life. Instead, it's about bringing joy and pleasure to those aspects. Few things could exemplify this way of thinking better than a café in a laundromat. Wherever you are, whatever you are doing, hygge can always be found or conjured up there. And when everyone engages in activities they may not like but finds a way to enjoy them anyway, society in general can be positively impacted.

CHAPTER 13:

THE IMPACT OF HYGGE ON SOCIETY

If hygge can significantly impact an individual, then it can also impact society. After all, society is made up of individuals; therefore, anything that affects many individuals will—by nature—also affect society. Hygge is no exception to this rippling. As mentioned earlier in this book, Denmark has a long-standing tradition of ranking in the top three countries in the world in terms of overall happiness, and it is not a coincidence. After all, one might expect Denmark to rank far lower on the charts due to a plethora of social and environmental factors. For starters, the weather in Denmark is darker and colder than in most other countries. These conditions tend to worsen depression and anxiety rather than generate happiness.

Additionally, Denmark does not have a booming consumerist society—you won't find endless shopping malls and other places to buy the latest and greatest gadgets like you will in the UK or the US. Nor will you find a Hollywood scene of celebrities that take up significant space in the consciousness of the Danish populace to escape their day-to-day stresses. Yet, despite all of these factors, Denmark consistently ranks among the top three countries in terms of happiness, reaching the number one spot as often as not. Can hygge really be the reason behind this sustained happiness? In short, yes, it can. And I'm going to discuss with you why.

To understand how hygge improves an entire society's happiness, we must first examine the things that hygge replaces. We have already mentioned the vicious cycle of consumerism. No object can ever bring true happiness and satisfaction; it is experiences that bring authentic joy to a person's life. That is why hygge is so effective at establishing and maintaining happiness, not only on the individual level but also on the social level. By focusing on experience rather than possessions, hygge can rescue a person from the endless cycle of consumerism and restore a genuine sense of happiness and contentment. However, this is only possible when someone begins to appreciate the simple pleasures in life. When most individuals in a community share this experience of appreciation, it begins to shape the social dynamic in an authentic way. Now, instead of streets full of people who are stressed out and eager to get their next consumer "fix," you have streets full of people who enjoy day-to-day life and understand and appreciate the things that are truly important in life. You will see streets where people move around more slowly, are less stressed and are focused on what they are doing rather than on the next thing.

As bad as the emptiness and inadequacy many people experience due to consumerism is, this way of living is only half of the problem. The other half of the problem is the crushing debt that so many people accrue in their attempts to fill their lives with the products and services that promise to bring them the happiness they crave. It is no secret that the economies in the West are debt-based, meaning that most people have debts rather than savings. Thus, not only does consumerism cause a sense of inadequacy and a sense of unfulfillment, but it also destroys the financial security that most people work so hard to achieve. Now, instead of a bank account full of retirement savings, the average Westerner has a storage shed full of unwanted and unused items that will never provide the joy and happiness that the consumerist world promised to them. Having all this stuff results in nothing but stress and anxiety, and the very real feeling that you do not have the money to get the things you need but cannot afford and a home full of clutter and junk. Danish people don't tend to waste their money on needless junk that only takes up space, and it wouldn't be incorrect to attribute this phenomenon to the hygge lifestyle. Instead, Danes tend to spend a larger portion of their money on quality time with friends, family, and loved ones. This quality time brings the joy and fulfillment that consumerism promises yet always fails to deliver. As a result, the average Dane has a contented heart and a solvent bank account, meaning that their financial stress levels are all but non-existent compared to those in consumerist societies.

Let it be known that I do not want to minimize the debt many people fall into, even if they live modestly possessions-wise. There are expensive mortgages, car payments, and colossal student loan debt in the USA and many other countries. However, my point is that so many of us still purchase things we either do not need or cannot afford, leading to further stress, anxiety, and financial hardship. Hey, maybe a hygge activity could be selling all the stuff you have but do not need or donating clothes you never wear to charities. Carrying out these activities would both lighten your load of material goods and either bring you some money or make you feel good that you are making a positive difference for others.

So, the impact that this economic security has on the individual is obvious, but how does this affect society as a whole? One significant difference between Danish society and American society is the amount of importance placed on work. Since the average Dane has all that they need to live a comfortable, happy, content life, they don't tend to have the desire to make more and more money, unlike many of their American counterparts. This attitude strongly affects how Danes view their work. Rather than centering their life and activities around work, Danish people tend to center on their whole lives and recognize that work merely comprises one aspect of it. They still have a schedule to work by, and they still have to work well in order to earn a paycheck. However, they don't tend to feel the need to be on standby 24 hours a day, seven days a week like so many Americans sadly are. Additionally, businesses aren't in such fierce competition with each other since the mentality of needing to be number one simply doesn't exist. Rather than needing to be the best, businesses recognize the importance of being a part of a greater whole, and their CEOs recognize they occupy a symbiotic place as just one part of the human world.

Being a part of the greater whole is a fundamental aspect of hygge in itself. By focusing on family and loved ones, the individual rediscovers their place in the grand scheme of things. Individual success and dominance will no longer be a way of life, and instead, cooperation, togetherness, and a sense of collective well-being take root. Thus, the stress and anxiety of always needing to be number one are entirely removed, replaced by a sense of satisfaction and gratitude for life in general. This permeates every level of society, shaping such things as work/life balance, political accountability, and even fiscal responsibility.

Another way in which hygge positively impacts society as a whole is that, by eliminating hyper-consumerism, it significantly reduces the waste we create—to the benefit of the planet we all call home. While consumerist societies can boast of substantial production numbers and sales figures, they have to also admit to overwhelming amounts of waste. Some of this waste is the result of more items being produced than are purchased. However, the vast majority of it results from perfectly good items being discarded to make room for the latest and greatest 'stuff' available. More and more electronics, clothing, automobiles, and other items are discarded year after year for no other reason than they simply aren't chic or up-to-date enough. The fact that they are in perfect working order never seems to matter at all. This rampant degree of waste only serves to compound our ever-present environmental nightmare. After all, where do you begin to put things that simply won't decompose over the course of time? Plastics, glass, metal components, and other parts constructed from non-biodegradable materials are what are used to create countless electronic items such as smartphones, computers, and tablets. Subsequently, when a phone is thrown away, it will take up space for hundreds if not thousands of years. Multiply that by millions of people per year, and you have yet another contribution to environmental disaster. And this environmental catastrophe is where a societal hygge mindset comes to the rescue yet again.

Since hygge takes the focus off consumerism, the average person living hygge will use a phone, laptop, and the like until they are no longer functioning. When you multiply this by the number of people in society, you could reduce overall waste production exponentially. After all, instead of buying a new phone each year, or even worse, every few months, the average Dane will buy a new phone every three to five years or more. The same goes for every other electronic device that they own. Chances are, the average Dane doesn't own as many electronic components to start with, since they don't see the same need for them. This means that Denmark's environment is far safer and cleaner because non-biodegradable trash has been limited significantly.

Hygge can have several other positive effects on a society's environment. First and foremost is a reduction in carbon emissions. Since activities such as walking and bicycling are often considered hygge, the amount of pollution caused by driving cars is significantly reduced in a hygge society. There's less need to own a car in a place like Denmark. When walking and bicycling are seen as viable alternatives to driving, even people who own cars will drive them less and keep the same one longer. This helps to keep the air considerably cleaner. Fewer cars also mean that fewer roads are required, meaning fewer disruptive construction projects. Additionally, fewer cars mean fewer parking lots are needed, which keeps the rural and urban landscapes far more visually appealing.

Another way that hygge helps the environment is to create a greater sense of appreciation for one's surroundings. When people take the time to enjoy a walk in the woods, they will be a lot less likely to cut the forest down in order to build a new shopping complex. Furthermore, when people find happiness and pleasure in their surroundings, they also tend to care for those surroundings better. Litter, pollution, over-development, and other harmful acts against nature are not accepted in hygge societies. Not only does this create an environment that is more harmonious with nature, but one that is healthier for people and all living things. Nature reduces stress and anxiety. Therefore, a nature-friendly environment will also be relaxing and calming for anyone living there.

Furthermore, the physical health benefits of a nature-friendly environment are highly significant. Better air quality, reduced noise pollution, and cleaner water are all abundant in places that protect and appreciate nature. Thus, when a society takes on a hygge approach to life, the symbiotic relationship between humanity and nature is maintained or restored.

Finally, there is the impact of hygge on crime and social disorder. While crime will exist in every society to some degree, crime rates are much lower in societies where hygge is a normal way of life. This is particularly true in the case of violent crime. Studies have shown that stress, anxiety, and the feeling of isolation and being alone are significant factors that contribute to crime in all forms, but especially violent crime. That said, it stands to reason that any society where a hygge lifestyle reduces these factors will have a significantly lower rate of crime as a result. Not only is crime lower in Denmark overall, but violent crime is all but non-existent compared to what it is in non-hygge Western societies. The importance of reducing stress and increasing life-satisfaction in an individual cannot be overstated. Any person who is generally happier with life will be far less likely to break any laws, as they will have less motivation to do so. When you take that to the social level, the numbers speak for themselves. In terms of non-violent crimes, Denmark ranks between 10th and 25th in the world, depending on the specific crime. In terms of violent crimes, Denmark ranks as low as 104th in the world. The vast spread between being in the top three happiest countries and being 104th for violent crime is no coincidence. It is a direct consequence of hygge being practiced on a societal and national level. And, once a society and a country are as hygge as possible, that can affect the entire world.

CHAPTER 14:

THE IMPACT OF HYGGE ON THE WORLD

So far, we have learned about the impact of hygge on the individual and an entire society. Since society comprises of individuals, if hygge can increase an individual's happiness, and most people in a given society practice hygge, then it could be assumed that a particular society would become happier in general. We have also seen how hygge can affect other aspects of society as well, including financial stability, environmental well-being, and a whole host of other critical measures. If a society is happier, then the world is that much happier. If a society can spread its positive way of life to other societies, the world will be even happier! Therefore, it is beyond dispute that hygge has a real impact on both an individual level and a collective level. The only question left to answer is just how far the effects of hygge can reach. If hygge can improve a person's life and a society, can it also improve the world at large? Can hygge provide the answers that humanity so desperately needs at this vital moment of human history? Based on what we have discovered so far, the answer to that question is a resounding "yes." After all, just as society is made up of a large number of individuals, so too, the world is made up of a large number of societies. Therefore, if the impact of hygge on the individual can influence society, then the impact of hygge on society should be able to influence the world. That influence could, in fact, be the very thing that humanity needs in order to restore peace and prosperity to a world suffering in turmoil. Therefore, it is essential to recognize yourself as one of the pieces in the sizeable hygge puzzle. By implementing hygge, you become that much more of a positive influence on the world around you.

In order to understand the changes that hygge could bring to the world, it is essential first to understand the problems that the world currently struggles with. If you were to ask the average person what one thing they would change about the world if they had a magic wand, the chances are most would eliminate war. War has dominated human history, and it has only gotten worse due to sophisticated weaponry. The 20th century saw the deadliest conflicts the world had ever seen, and over 108 million people died due to conflict in this 100-year span. Every corner of the world is caught up in a conflict of one size or another even right now. This state of war is the antithesis of the serene and peaceful environment that hygge can create and the harmony that the lifestyle promises. Just as hygge can help a single person remove stress and anxiety from their life, and thus live a life of inner and outer peace, hygge could also remove much of the hatred and strife that causes nations and groups to go to war with each other in the first place. After all, one of the main aspects of hygge is the quest for pleasure and comfort. When an individual seeks out happy moments, not only do they find happiness and thus relieve stress, but they also change their outlook on life in general. Rather than looking for reasons to complain or start a fight, a person practicing hygge will look for opportunities to be happy and experience comfort. Anyone looking to be happy will be far less likely to engage in a conflict of any sort. When you multiply this to the collective world level, this would mean that countries would spend their time and energy on finding pleasure and contentment rather than trying to dominate and control the rest of the planet. Any country that spent its resources searching for ways for its entire population to be comfortable and happy would totally oppose anything that would stand in the way of that ideal. Since war and conflict would undermine the happiness (and fun) the people in a country could experience, it makes sense that a country practicing hygge would strongly avoid anything that would lead to war or conflict. Needless to say, that would be a far different reality than the one we face in the world today. However, as individuals, it is up to us to change that and bring more peace to the world at large.

In fact, we can easily draw a correlation between war and the overall focus of a nation, specifically its cultural value system. Throughout history, it is a common theme that nations that fixated on depriving themselves of worldly pleasures were far more likely to engage in a global conflict in one form or another. This is likely due to the suppression of their desires, which leads to an inner conflict, which is then projected onto the outside world. Sometimes this conflict would take the shape of an actual war with another developed nation, such as wars between Britain and France, or Britain and Spain, whereas other times, this conflict would take the shape of wars of conquest, such as the Spanish conquest of the New World. This trend is also evident in more recent times, such as in World War II. When you examine Germany and Japan's cultural values, you see the common thread of leaving behind a certain level of worldly pleasure for devotion to duty and service to the state. The idea wasn't to find happiness in life but rather to promote nationalism and racial supremacy. This fixation on national identity, specifically as being superior to other nations and races, gave rise to the justification for fighting wars of conquest and subjugation over the supposedly 'inferior' peoples of Earth. Rather than being an isolated incident, this direct relationship between sacrifice and violence can be seen throughout human history. Therefore, in the way that a certain mindset can bring about conflict, war, and strife, another mindset can bring about peace, love, and harmony. If people and nations in the 20th century were more focused on the wellbeing of all through a hygge mindset, maybe everything would have been different. But that wasn't the reality. However, we all have a chance to make things better for the world today by changing our mindsets as individuals.

In contrast to early- and mid-20th century Germany and Japan, you can look at nations that focus on finding pleasure and joy in life and will find cultures that are far less willing to engage in a war of any kind. It is of little wonder that the Scandinavian countries, specifically Denmark, have been off the radar in terms of global conflicts for a considerable length of time. While some might argue that Denmark's size is what keeps them from being a global threat, it would be worth pointing out that Great Britain, the Netherlands, and Japan are not too dissimilar in terms of size. Yet, all of these countries have involved themselves in numerous global conflicts over the past few centuries. When it comes to war, one simple rule of thumb prevails—"Where there's a will, there's a way." The size of a nation doesn't necessarily dictate whether or not that nation will be capable of waging war on another. Rather, the heart of a nation determines that. It also goes with the consumerist mindset that some countries wage war. They want more: more riches, more territories, and more influence on the global stage. For example at its peak, the British Empire ruled more than 1/3 of the world—to do so requires a level of war-waging and subjecting other people to their rule. They were focused on expansion and conquest, not peace for all. Thus, countries that focus on finding happiness and peace in day-to-day life, regardless of size, are the ones that will avoid conflict at virtually all costs.

Denmark is a good example. Its current status as the seat of hygge—much like Tibet is the seat of Buddhism—means that the nation as a whole has absolutely no interest in causing harm or suffering, either to its own people or the other people in the world at large. It is the prime example of a nation embracing peace and happiness. Again, they are focused on experience, no accumulating more land or things.

Just to drive the point home in a way that might be easier to measure, consider the fact that Denmark was one of the countries of origin for the infamous Vikings, who engaged in global warfare of various forms several centuries ago. They engaged in nefarious war practices—like pillaging villages—and they were also interested in power, control, and dominance. The fact that the same country that helped create the Viking culture also launched the hygge culture shows just how significant the hygge lifestyle is in transforming a society and a people. After all, Denmark is a modern-day beacon of happiness and peace, a far cry from their reputation in the ninth century. Now, rather than being the nation of ruthless, blood-thirsty warriors wielding swords and axes, Denmark is a nation of happiness, pleasure, and warmth (the people, not the climate!).

The reason the Danes are synonymous with these things alongside the rise in popularity of the hygge tradition is no mere coincidence. Rather, it demonstrates the very real correlation between hygge and the national identity of 21st century Denmark. Imagine, if one country can reinvent itself through adoption of hygge, how different the world could become if every country were to do the same? If instead of trying to be the best and trying to dominate others, countries would simply seek for their citizens pleasure in day-to-day life—all war, turmoil, and strife could come to an end. If we were to create peace and harmony in our own lives, how transformative could these practices improve others' lives?

Hygge could also help eliminate various other threats to the world in general. One such threat is the destruction of the environment. While there are several reasons the planet is undergoing environmental challenges of different forms, humankind's exploitation of minerals and other natural resources is perhaps the most significant. It is certainly the most controllable, and the one that would be directly impacted if the world as a whole started practicing hygge. Since hygge reduces the influence of materialism and consumerism, it makes sense that if the world followed the hygge way of life, then the need to extract minerals and raw materials would decrease exponentially.

Furthermore, the excess waste dumped into landfills would be reduced, resulting in the environment being protected 'at both ends' of the production-to-dumping lifecycle. Not only would the environment not be depleted of resources, but it would also not be a dumping ground for humanity's trash. Unfortunately, since many countries remain rooted in hyper-consumerism, it seems that the environment is a long way from being cared for the way that it both deserves and needs. However, you only have to look at countries like Denmark, where consumerism is not the way of life, to see how the environment could be improved if more of the world took on the lifestyle of hygge. Through the actions of each of us reducing our focus on material goods, we could help the environment monumentally. Exchanging consumerist goods for experiences may just be the step we need to take to save the planet.

Another way the environment would benefit from hygge is that humanity would stop treating it as unimportant, and perhaps more as a single, living organism or ecosystem. The number one reason so many industries continue to dump waste and toxic materials into the rivers and oceans is that they simply have lost all sense of respect and admiration for nature. Profit and shortcuts are the sole focus of many corporations that neglect to consider the damage done to the planet. But since hygge promotes spending time in nature in order to find peace and happiness, it ultimately fosters a greater love and appreciation for nature. The result will be a more symbiotic relationship between humankind and the environment, which will lead to a new appreciation of the natural world. When this relationship is restored, then the abuses against nature and the environment will come to an end. No person or entity that appreciates nature would continue to poison the rivers and oceans with waste material.

Additionally, the need for oil and gas would be reduced exponentially as more and more people began to use less intrusive forms of transportation than those requiring fossil fuels. Not only would this help protect the environment from constant drilling and mining, but it would also help clean the air of the carbon gasses that are causing all sorts of environmental problems. Whether you accept the science or not, the fact is that the climate on this planet is changing. If more of the world would respect and protect nature, as the hygge lifestyle encourages, then it is possible that this threat could be stopped before it is too late. We are near the point of no return, so we must act now to not step over the line. There is so little time, so immediate action is imperative.

Finally, there is the impact that hygge could have on things such as famine, disease, and other such dangers that threaten the lives of millions. While hygge isn't necessarily rooted in helping other people—although it can be for you—it does help foster a greater sense of community. This is particularly true in terms of family. By spending more time with family and friends, a person can hardly turn a blind eye to when members of their inner circle are struggling in life. It makes sense that as your friends and family become more important to you that you would want to help them whenever possible. Again, this isn't necessarily a direct goal of hygge, but it is a very real side effect of practicing a hygge lifestyle. If this attitude were taken to a global level, nations worldwide would put forth a greater effort to lend assistance to places hit by famine, disease, and natural disasters. Rather than making a token effort for appearance's sake, countries would strive to solve the problems and bring lasting relief to those affected. This would be a global manifestation of the hygge sense of family and community. By embracing every nation as a part of the global family, no country would be able to stand by idly while the populace of another nation suffered and died.

Furthermore, since consumerism and greed are replaced by generosity and gratitude through hygge, it makes sense that each nation's leaders and citizens would find joy in healing the planet. Instead of using humanitarian efforts to exert political leverage, nations would use them to increase all people's happiness and contentment. All in all, hygge could turn the world into a place where humanity respects nature, preserves peace, and promotes happiness and well-being for all people and life on planet Earth.

CONCLUSION

When it comes to defining, categorizing, and identifying a feeling of hygge, the term "lifestyle" does not quite capture it. With many lifestyles, there are certain rules, strategies, practices, and mantras. Hygge, however, does not encompass rules, regulations, products, or even stereotypical mantras. It encompasses a *feeling*. This is the reason the Scandinavian word is untranslatable in many countries. For areas of the world that base their ideas of success, wealth, and growth on personal assets and analyzed statistics, the idea of utilizing emotion to somehow judge personal growth on these scales is foreign and nonsensical. In many countries and cultures, the amount of land one owns or even the amount of money in the bank is how success in life is measured.

Not so with some cultures, especially the Danish culture, but also the Nordic culture at large. That is the difference.

So, how do you take a word that points to a completely different ruler of measurement for success and define it in a culture that sees that same ruler as a foreign concept?

It's easy: you simply promote the idea of self-awareness.

Being self-aware in the lifestyle of hygge is essential, especially for those raised in a culture in which emotion is something to cast off to the side in favor of other things (or a 'stiff upper lip,' as the British call it). For those raised in cultures where emotion and feelings are even considered one's downfall, the lifestyle of hygge can be almost impossible to understand, much less promote.

But to people in these types of cultures, hygge can be the most freeing and healthy lifestyle they can choose to live. If individuals in these cultures shift their mindsets, they may plant the seeds of a more open society.

Hygge is not merely the promotion of relaxation and comfort, though that is how one gauges whether or not hygge is being achieved. Promoting these aspects of life enable inward health, from physical healing to mental rejuvenation. The reduction of stresses and anxieties helps the body heal from the damage that stress induces over long periods of time. Stress reduction reduces levels of damaging chemicals, which can elicit everything from life-threatening fatigue to chronic, debilitating migraines. Allowing the body to relax enables organs to filter the cortisol from the bloodstream and muscle tissue so that automatic immune responses can kick into overdrive and begin to repair the body.

Reducing stress and anxieties also promotes mental health. Many cases of depression, including the seasonal variety, can be traced back to an overflow of cortisol in the body, specifically for those who suffer from chronic migraines that create lesions in the brain that hamper neurotransmitter receptors. Lesions prevent those synapses and neurons from absorbing the chemicals the brain needs to balance itself. This imbalance results in a slew of issues because of an overload of cortisol in response to constant stressors.

Emotional health is also impacted positively by a hygge lifestyle. All of these issues that stem from debilitated physical and mental health ultimately affect someone emotionally. Chemical imbalances can create mood swings that lead to mounting self-consciousness, anxiety, and panic attacks. These attacks promote more bodily harm, which in turn causes a negative reel of thoughts to play out repeatedly in someone's head, and the cyclical process ultimately destroys all three facets of personal health. This happens all because of a chronic surge of cortisol in their systems.

Hygge is driven by one guideline and one guideline alone: "Treat yourself with kindness." In a world where people are constantly distracted with things that seem more important than their overall health, it is hard to convey the importance of recognizing that you are the only one responsible for taking care of yourself. We all watch romantic lifetime movie marathons where one character is ultimately abusing themselves in some way until another character swoops in, recognizes all of their faults, throws themselves into fixing the other, and then they fall in love and live happily ever after. And while that is a popular romantic notion, it harbors an extremely dangerous message: that someone else will come along and take care of you eventually.

And most often, that is not the case.

Hygge is about self-care. Hygge promotes the idea of relaxation and the idea of being strong enough to take care of oneself. It promotes the foundation of putting yourself first and conceals it under a mask of "you deserve this." Not only do you deserve it, but you also are entitled to it, yet it is up to you to go out there and earn it. With the mounting stresses this life will ultimately dole out to every single person on this planet, you are entitled to downtime during which the only focus is on you. There is a reason why hair salons, spas, movie theaters, concerts, stage productions, and even some vacation packages can charge as much as they do and get away with it. They understand people's insatiable desire to relax and "get away from it all."

However, the idea that hundreds, or even thousands, of dollars need to be spent to achieve the experience of unwinding and relaxing is far from the truth. Media advertising campaigns have trained us to expect high prices depending on the level of relaxation and pampering we wish, and even those decisions can become stressful. The sheer amount of money spent can turn a relaxing vacation into yet another stressful event in someone's life.

That is not the type of relaxation hygge promotes.

Instead, hygge focuses on ordinary personal necessities and helps translate them into personal enjoyment exercises. If someone's innermost need is to sleep, then hygge suggests doing something like purchasing that comfortable pajama set you have been eyeballing or drinking a warm cup of tea before you retire for the night. If someone's innermost need is to stay warm during the winter, hygge promotes long, hot showers or baths and warm, comfortable blankets. Suppose someone's innermost need is to be around friends and partake in uproarious laughter. In that case, hygge promotes watching a comedy movie with friends or enjoying a glass of wine over a great conversation in a comfortable room. Hygge can be implemented at all times, anywhere, and fits any budget.

In other words, hygge does not promote spending money to relax; it promotes enhancing atmospheres already accessible to us that aid in relaxation.

For Danes, hygge is a natural necessity. Just as constantly being available for a job is common in many cultures, consistent hygge is common in Danish culture. Danes decorate their apartments, purchase their homes, and even arrange family events with the idea of hygge in mind. For many in the Danish culture, doing this type of thing is natural and requires little to no additional thought. It is why many Danes have just as hard a time explaining it as many cultures do understanding it: because it is so natural and ingrained, it is hard for them to understand that not everyone lives this way.

For example, if someone came up to you and asked you to define the word "living," what would you say? Perhaps someone has asked you what it means or how you do it... what would you tell them? Would you say that "living" means getting up and breathing? Or that "living" means going out and enjoying life? Or that "living" even means enjoying what life has to offer? If you ask ten different people, you will acquire ten different answers, and that is what would happen if you asked ten Danes to define the word "hygge."

You would get ten different answers, not because it is rare and misunderstood, but because it is common *and* personal.

When it comes down to it, hygge is a feeling generated by a particular surrounding based solely on the interpreter of the situation. What one person finds comforting, another will find annoying or bothersome. What one person finds idiotic, another might find funny. And what one person finds beautiful, another might find unattractive. Hygge incorporates just as much diversity as the people implementing the lifestyle, and that is the beauty of the entire concept: rules and regulations do not apply. Dollar amounts and income status do not apply. It is not confined to a specific country or race or gender, or sexual orientation. It is merely about how the person experiencing life interprets any particular experience emotionally.

That is what hygge truly is: a personal experience between yourself and relaxation.

All this lifestyle does is promote self-care in a way many people neglect. All this lifestyle promises is to make sure you are the healthiest you can be. All this lifestyle is about is to make you happy.

You do not work for this lifestyle; it works for you.

And that is its true, unadulterated beauty.

Welcome to the world of hygge. It's time to enjoy your new standard of living!

THANKS FOR READING

I really hope you enjoyed this book, and most of all – got more value from it than you had to give.

It would mean a lot to me if you left an Amazon review – I will reply to all questions asked!

Simply find this book on Amazon, scroll to the reviews section, and click "Write a customer review".

Or please visit www.pristinepublish.com/hyggebundlereview to leave a review

Be sure to check out my email list, where I am constantly adding tons of value.

The best way to get on the list currently is by visiting www.pristinepublish.com and entering your email.

Here I'll provide actionable information that aims to improve your enjoyment of life.

I'll update you on my latest books and I'll even send free e-books that I think you'll find useful.

Kindest regards,

Olivia Telford

THE ART OF MINIMALISM

A SIMPLE GUIDE TO DECLUTTER AND ORGANIZE YOUR LIFE

Olivia Telford

.

CONTENTS

INTRODUCTION

Greetings readers! First, I want to thank you for purchasing my book, as it has always been my lifelong passion to help others. In my moments of despair, when I didn't think there was any hope, I couldn't even fathom the idea of one day being able to turn my mess into a message. However, with much determination, study, and application of what I have learned, and experiencing a dramatic transformation in my life, I am now able to pass on what I have learned and help others live a better life by becoming the best version of themselves. Second, I want to congratulate you for taking the bold step towards change, because I can tell you from my own personal experience that it is not easy.

We live in a world that tells us that in order to be happy we must acquire more goods. Everywhere we look and everywhere we turn we are bombarded with images of what it means to be prosperous and successful, but what ends up happening is that we become overwhelmed with the meaningless goods we have acquired. Clutter in the home creates disorder, and disorder in the home creates chaos in our lives.

In this book you will learn that there is much more to clutter than you thought. Not only am I going to teach you how to eliminate clutter from your home, but also how to eliminate clutter from your relationships, emotions, and much more, so that you can live the happy and prosperous life that you know you deserve!

In order to maximize the value you receive from this book, I highly encourage you to join our tight-knit community on Facebook. Here you will be able to connect and share with other like-minded Minimalists to continue your growth.

Taking this journey alone is not recommended, and this can be an excellent network for you.

It would be great to connect with you there,

Olivia Telford

To Join, Visit:
www.pristinepublish.com/hyggegroup

WHAT OTHERS ARE SAYING ABOUT *THE ART OF MINIMALISM*

"Olivia Telford's The Art of Minimalism shares an invaluable lesson about redesigning your life top to bottom. She redirects you from seeking happiness in consumerism and points you towards relationships, experiences, and soul care –places that you will find life and true lasting happiness. It has made me realize how all the stuff I own has been holding me back from pursuing my dreams. A truly wonderful book that can change your life and keep you organized for years to come."

— Daniel Walter, author of 10-Minute Focus: 25 Habits for Mastering Your Concentration and Eliminating Distractions

"This is an incredible book that shows you how powerful it is to live with less. Highly recommend."

— Bella Jean, author of The Forever In Between: A Historical Western Romance Book

"If you are looking to declutter and experience the joys of peace, contentment and purposeful living than this is the book for you. In The Art of Minimalism you will find comprehensive and straightforward techniques you can use today to instantly improve your home and wellbeing. After reading this book, I've never felt more organized, stress free and productive. Whether you've tried minimalism before or are brand new to it, this is the perfect guide."

— Judy Dyer, author of Empath: A Complete Guide
for Developing Your Gift and Finding Your Sense of Self

CHAPTER 1:

START BY MAKING YOUR BED

I can already hear you…"Start by making your bed?!" It sounds absolutely ridiculous, doesn't it? But did you know that this is the first lesson that the people who protect your country learn when they enter the military? It sounds completely backward— there is a global crisis of terrorism but bed making is a priority! No matter what country you are in, before the military trains their soldiers to fight on the battlefield, they train them how to make their beds. And I mean rigorous training. If there is ever such thing as a bed making competition, a soldier will win it every time. Why are they trained to make their beds with proper forty-five-degree hospital corners? Is the opposition going to be impressed by their ability to bounce a quarter off the bed? No! The purpose is to instill a habit of excellence into the soldiers. Human beings are creatures of habit—if a person thinks it's okay to leave trash in his car, he will leave it in any car he sits in because that's just what he does. The bottom line is that it's the smallest habits that count. They determine how you are going to do everything else in life. In other words, if a soldier can't make his bed, he has no business defending his country.

Imagine walking into the barracks of the American Army and seeing a line of unmade beds, clothes all over the floor, and the place just looking like an overall hot mess. How much faith would you have in the military? None, right? Your first thought would be, if they can't keep their own living space clean, how can they safeguard the country? If you can't be bothered to make your bed, you won't be bothered when it comes to loading your rifle. A cluttered environment is a reflection of a cluttered mind. I generally find it pretty easy to judge where a person is mentally when I walk into their house. This is why there is so much importance placed on attention to' detail in every area of a soldier's training. In the military, beds are called racks, and making a rack in a specific way is not just for cleanliness, but also to ensure that all the soldiers are on the same page.

Navy Seal Admiral Bill McRaven gave a speech at the University of Texas where he spoke about the 10 lessons he learned while he was being trained as a SEAL. It sounded awfully strange to hear such a strong and accomplished man state that he got to where he is today because of something as simple as making his bed! He went on to state that making your bed in the morning is an accomplishment—it gives you a sense of pride that you have achieved something for that day. It also provides momentum and additional encouragement to move onto completing other tasks. Keeping your house in order is not the only thing that's important here; the standards you set for yourself and how much respect you have for yourself and your family is made clear by your environment.

It is also important to note that this is not about pursuing perfection but excellence. People who do things in a spirit of excellence, do mundane, ordinary everyday tasks in an extraordinary way.

The first directive I am giving you in your journey to personal growth is to clean yourself up! I know, this doesn't sound very exciting and it's certainly not the stuff that movies are made of. In fact, it probably sounds pretty foolish if you are someone who's got big dreams, but it's important. The idea here is that if you are faithful with the small things, you will be faithful with the big things. And if you are dishonest with the small things, you will be dishonest with the big things. If you can't get your house in order, how can you get anything else in your life in order? If you want to get anywhere in life, you must adopt a standard of excellence—this is how you prepare for success.

Remember, the way you keep your house is the way you will keep everything else in your life. The standard of excellence you keep is all about preparing yourself for greatness; where you go next in your life is always connected to what you are doing now. Excellence is the key that opens doors of opportunities that will plant your feet on the path to success.

It's interesting how we can become immune to clutter, acclimated to debris, and adjusted to junk. We become so complacent around things that once got on our nerves to no end, that we eventually end up ignoring it as if the clutter is no longer visible. Close your eyes and imagine that you want to sell your house, so you put it on the market in the state that it's in today. Who do you think is going to buy it? No one! It will stay on the market until you clean it up.

There are no short cuts in life—whatever you want is going to take a lot of work, because all great things take time. The question is, are you prepared to put the effort in? Not only to get there but to maintain it. You see, the universe has to know that it can trust you before it gives you what you want. So, if you are only going to keep up your standard of excellence for one month and then slip back into your old habits, don't expect to move forward in life. You will stay stuck in the same old rut until excellence becomes a normal part of your life. The problem is that the majority of people are impatient—the woman who wants a body like Jennifer Lopez can't expect to work out for a few hours and hope to see results. It doesn't work like that, and when people don't see immediate results, they revert back to old habits. Maybe you are like this yourself, or you have a friend like it—for the past two years they have gone on every diet under the sun, but they are still overweight. That's because they never stick to anything long enough to see results.

A lot of people believe that there is no point in making your bed in the morning because you are only going to get back into it at night. May I submit to you that every time you make your bed in the morning you are preparing for greatness.

Most people don't see the point of washing the dishes before they go to bed; after all, they are only going to use more dishes in the morning. May I submit to you that every time you wash the dishes before you go to bed, you are preparing for greatness.

Most people don't see the point in hanging their clothes up when they take them off because they are only going to wear them again the next day. May I submit to you that every time you hang your clothes up in the evening, you are preparing for greatness.

There is a possibility that, like a petulant teenager, you believe that these things are irrelevant, but let me remind you again that it's these small habits and personal standards of excellence that will determine how well you do everything else in life.

CHAPTER 2:

WHAT EXACTLY IS DECLUTTERING?

T here is nothing complicated about decluttering. It is a simple process that involves getting rid of the things in your house that you don't need. However, the funny thing is that there are many people who have no idea what decluttering is—their idea of a clear-out is moving things around and making them look neat. That, my friend, is not decluttering! Neither is it buying a new wardrobe, shelves, or drawers and stacking away the things you don't want, and neither is it organizing or filing. You see, when you've shifted things around, organized, or hidden all of your unused items, they are still there taking up unnecessary space, just in a different way. When it comes to decluttering, your focus should be on one thing, and that is getting what you don't need out of the house.

When you do this, not only will you feel as if a weight has been lifted off your shoulders, you will feel that a weight has also been lifted off your home. You will find that your life is much easier, and your home will function much better. Think about it like this, anything in your home that you feel you have no control over is considered clutter. Once you have completed the decluttering process, that should be the yardstick you use to judge whether you are accumulating too many things again.

May I warn you that this process is not going to be easy; in fact, it is very overwhelming, which is why a lot of people choose to rearrange things instead of getting rid of them—it eliminates the decision-making process. However, the best way to overcome this is just to get on with it. Just don't dive right in at the deep end—start with the small things first. For example, a drawer in your bedroom or office, just open it and start throwing out the things you don't need. Once you have made some space and you realize how much better it looks, and how much better it makes you feel, you will be inspired to continue.

It's Not the Size of Your Home—It's You!

I believe that many people move from their home unnecessarily because of all the stuff they've accumulated over the years—their house starts to look like a thrift store. The next thing you know, they are moving into a bigger house, one with more storage space and more rooms; but guess what happens? They pack the house with more things they don't need, and the house ends up looking no different than the one they've just moved out of. Once you finally stop using the spaces you should be the most comfortable in to store the things you don't really need, you will be much happier. In fact, you will start finding rooms and spaces in your home that you didn't know existed! Almost like magic, your house will become bigger than you thought it was.

Stop Putting Your Stuff Before Your Space

What's your favorite comfort food? (Please bear with me a moment, I'm going somewhere with this!) Well, mine is whipped vanilla ice cream (the type you got when you were a kid from the ice-cream van) with strawberry juice, nuts, and 2 chocolate flakes poked into the top! The thought of it makes my mouth water! But when I'm stuck in a rut, depressed, or stressed out, I go and find the ice cream man and get me some ice cream. My point is that even though comfort food tastes delicious, it's typically bad for you, and we would all be much better off if we turned to fruit and vegetables for comfort food instead, but hey—wishful thinking right!

My point is that clutter is "comfort food" for some people. Think about the last time you ate some comfort food—it felt really good while you were eating it right? But afterward, you didn't feel so great. Not only because the food was finished but because you knew you were going to put on some extra pounds, and those jeans you just bought would no longer fit. So, when you go to wear those skinny jeans and realize they don't fit, you get frustrated, and that frustration makes you want to eat more comfort foods, so now you've gotten yourself into a vicious cycle that's difficult to break.

This is the same process that takes place when you are constantly buying things that you think you might need in the future. You walk through the store aisles grabbing things because you think they might be of some benefit to you or one of your family members somewhere down the line. However, two years pass, the things have collected an avalanche of dust, but you are still confident that you will use it one day. When you purchased the item, it felt great; but then when you try to clean and have no space, you start complaining that it's so difficult to clean your home! So just as the ice cream turns into frustration when the buttons start to pop, that pleasurable feeling of buying something turns into frustration when you find it difficult to clean or can't find the things you do need because the house is so full of things you don't need! Do you see the connection here?

You start looking at your pile of unnecessary items as even more valuable than the space that you need, simply because you have convinced yourself that you might need them one day. And like your comfort food, this is not healthy. Once you start going through your piles of stuff, you will realize that for every ten items that you don't need, there is only one item that you do need. Once you start getting rid of worthless things, you will find a new love, and that love is space!

WHERE DID ALL THIS STUFF COME FROM ANYWAY?

Once upon a time it was in our best interest to hoard things, resources were scarce, and you didn't know if you'd ever be able to get it again if you threw it out. After the Industrial Revolution, things started to change. You could easily get your hands on a variety of goods and they were relatively cheap. The brainiacs of the world began to invent things such as washing machines, dishwashers, and cars. Life was sweet, and people really didn't need anything else since they had so much leisure time to enjoy. This was when sales started to decline.

Moving onto World War II, the economy had changed and bumped heads with consumer contentment. So, the brainiacs put their heads together again to come up with a strategy to get people buying again, and we transitioned from being content with our dishwashers, washing machines, and cars to over-consumers and buying things that quite frankly, we don't need. What happened? The answer lies in the multi-billion-dollar advertising industry.

Today, it is impossible to walk past an empty store, people are always buying something new. Why? Because marketing companies hire geniuses to create enticing advertising campaigns to convince us to buy what we don't need. Not only that, but they are also using a clever technique called neuromarketing. Advertising companies employ neuroscientists to help them tap into the subconscious mind and shut down the area in the brain responsible for telling us that we don't need something. Instead, advertisements trigger the part of the brain that makes us feel that we are lacking something. Once we are in a state of vulnerability, we are presented with the thing that will fill the void and solve the problem. Are you single? That's probably because you don't have the right clothes to attract the right partner. But if you buy this $150 pair of jeans, you will have all the hot girls swarming around you like bees on honey.

Living a minimalist life requires that you take a break from impulse buying. It means that you are no longer a slave to advertising campaigns and that you have full control over your buying habits. The media is constantly sending us messages that we need more—you have to upgrade your phone, increase your credit limit, buy a newer model car, improve your wardrobe, and the list goes on! These messages are drilled into us and affirmed on every corner—children hear it at school and adults hear it at work. We hear it so much that we believe it, that's why kids cry and stamp their feet until they get the latest toy, and parents go into debt to keep up with the Joneses. But the fact is that you don't need any of these things, and you will realize this once you start living a minimalist life.

Imagine if these messages were reversed, and all we heard was, "Save 80 percent of your income so that you can retire at 40." People would start to believe it and take action towards it. But this message would never become mainstream because it doesn't benefit the bigwigs. They need us to spend our money and get into debt to keep their pockets fat.

CLUTTER IS A WASTE OF TIME, ENERGY, AND SPACE

What happens when you can't find something? No matter what it is, you are going to spend time and energy trying to find it. When your home is overflowing with things you don't use, you are taking up unnecessary space. A messy home can also make you feel frustrated, embarrassed, and anxious. Frustrated because you can never find anything, embarrassed because you see the looks on your friends' faces when they come to your house, and anxious because you are always worried that someone might ring the door at any moment.

You can change this way of living if you really want to. It's going to take time, dedication, and energy, but it will all be well spent. Have you ever stayed in a nice hotel? Do you remember that peaceful feeling when you first walked in? If not, Google one—just looking at how organized the room is gives you a sense of calm and well-being. When you stay in a hotel, you've got just about enough of everything to get you through your stay—one towel, one bar of soap, one book to read, and a few clothes. Life is easy because you don't have to deal with the stress of being surrounded by a bunch of possessions you don't need. What if you could transform the vacation version of you into the real you? The good news is that you can, and there's no time like the present.

Most people don't like tidying up, especially when it's a mammoth task. So, they keep putting it off until next weekend turns into next year! There is more to procrastination than meets the eye. At its core, it's rooted in fear. And when it comes to decluttering, there are certain possessions that can bring dormant emotions to the surface that we really don't want to deal with. In some cases, we have piled a month's worth of laundry on top of our emotions hoping to keep them buried.

Where you live is a reflection of who you are on the inside. When you declutter your home, you have to face parts of yourself that you were trying to ignore. So, to a certain extent, you need to prepare yourself for the emotional upheaval that is about to take place. If possessions were just possessions, getting rid of them wouldn't matter. But in some cases, they come with a whole heap of emotional baggage. But as Lao Tzu says, a journey of a thousand miles starts with one step, and once you take that first step, you will build momentum and start feeling a sense of freedom as you are released from your past.

Now, if you don't have a notebook, I want you to go out and buy one. Not just any old random notebook, a nice one. It might be in your favorite color or have a motivational quote on it, but you will know when you see it. It should be small enough for you to comfortably carry around with you. This will be your decluttering journal and you are going to use it to record your decluttering process—write down how you felt when you threw certain items away, how many bags you have donated to charity. How you felt when you finished your first room, then your second, how you felt after giving yourself that much-deserved reward, etc.

Studies have revealed that no matter how many toys children have, they end up playing with the same toy because they have too many to choose from and it confuses them. Well, children are not the only ones who have too many things, adults do too, and these unnecessary possessions are taking up too much energy, thought, space, and not to mention a waste of money, especially when none of them are providing any real benefit.

Sometimes it feels as if the items in our cupboards, on our shelves, garages, and lofts multiply as soon as we turn our backs!

One day, you just look at everything and wonder where it all came from.

Do you have so many things in your kitchen that you struggle to find the space to cook? What about the bathroom? Do you have to move things off the toilet seat when you need to use it? Is your wardrobe about to fall apart because it's so full?

How Do We Accumulate So Much Clutter?

Where does all this stuff come from anyway? Car boot sales, markets, Christmas presents we don't like, souvenirs, eBay, Amazon, Gumtree, and the list goes on. Most of what we now consider clutter doesn't start off that way—clutter is what it turns into when we stop using the items. Yes, there are some things we purchase that we only use once and toss to the side. But we do get some good usage out of the majority of things. So, a part of the problem is that we have a bad habit of buying things we don't really need, and the other half is that we don't know how to throw the things away that we no longer use. These things build up over the years, and when we realize we are running out of space, instead of giving things away or selling them, we buy storage boxes and stuff them in the bottom of wardrobes, in garages, and lofts.

Why do We Buy More Than We Need?

There are many reasons why we have developed a habit of buying more than we need.

Souvenirs: We go on vacation or to a town in our country we have never visited before and buy something small and cheap to remind us that we have been there.

Just in Case: Then there are moments when we know we don't need the item now, but we think we will use it later, so we buy it anyway. The problem is that we never end up using it.

We Think We Need It: We are often guilty of believing we need certain things when, in reality, we don't. Like the oven cleaner you just saw advertised on TV, but you already have one and just think that this one being advertised will give your oven an additional shine.

Self-Improvement: We have been conditioned to believe that the more we accumulate the better our lives will be. Or the better we will look.

A BIT OF HISTORY

Before World War II, most kitchens were clutter-free and cooking was done on a stove top or in the oven using a limited amount of pots and pans. The most popular kitchen item before WWII was the cast iron skillet, which could be used on the stove or placed in the oven. They were nonstick and were often inherited from parents or grandparents, meaning that they were very durable.

There was a huge leap in technological advancement after WWII and kitchen gadgets were among the many developments. The microwave oven was discovered by Percy Spencer. As the story goes, he actually discovered it by accident. Spencer was employed by a company called Raytheon who developed microwave transmitters. One day, he left a candy bar in his pocket while he was working on some equipment, and he noticed that it started melting. He decided to start experimenting with the equipment and discovered that microwaves could heat food.

Spencer went on to invent the first microwave oven, and the first thing he cooked in it was popcorn.

There is no denying the fact that the microwave was a great invention, but there is also no denying the fact that they take up space in the kitchen! The economic boom gave more people access to products such as refrigerators and freezers, which were only available to the wealthy before the war.

Technology continued to advance, and other equipment such as toasters, rice cookers, pressure cookers, and portable grills were now on the market. All of which took up space on kitchen work surfaces. Today we have pressure cookers that are controlled by smartphone apps!

The post-war period also led to a dramatic shift in our eating habits. More women had entered the workforce, and they had less time to cook. It was during this time that ready-made processed foods became popular. All of which are high in sugar, saturated fats, and carbohydrates. Many experts claim that there was also a steep increase in obesity during this time.

It appears that clutter is a modern-day issue, and more often than not you will hear grandparents complaining about the number of things we have in the home today. Think about it, if people didn't need all this stuff back then, why do we need it now?

CHAPTER 3:

GETTING ORGANIZED – THE BENEFITS

C lutter, mess, junk... whatever you want to call it, when you have no room it causes chaos. It's not just an eyesore, it's bad for your mental and physical well-being. A study conducted by the University of New Mexico discovered that family members felt uncomfortable in a cluttered home. Participants stated that they didn't feel as if it was a home and neither did they feel safe and secure. This relates to the psychologist Abraham Maslow's hierarchy of needs. He presents the basic human needs in pyramid form—our survival needs are at the base of the pyramid, all humans need adequate shelter, sleep, food, water, and homeostasis. He places financial stability and personal safety above this. Next is our need for love and acceptance within a group. At the top of the pyramid is what Maslow refers to as self-actualization, which means that you have fulfilled your potential and have become everything you were destined to be. However, before we arrive here, we must have fulfilled the desires at the bottom of the pyramid.

The home is what we would consider shelter; it is the place where we should feel safe and secure. Clutter makes it impossible to feel secure and therefore, there is a negative psychological impact associated with living in a messy house.

Studies have also found that a messy home is linked to bad eating habits. Think about it, who wants to cook in a kitchen with dishes stacked to the ceiling and trash everywhere? Getting takeout or snacking makes things easier when the kitchen is a mess. Bad eating habits then contribute to bad health, and the vicious cycle begins.

Studies have also found that a cluttered work environment has a negative effect on employee productivity. Clutter makes it difficult for employees to focus, slows down visual processing, and they are easily distracted because there is always something else to focus on other than their work. The brain finds it difficult to differentiate between relevant and irrelevant stimuli, and clutter is considered irrelevant stimuli, causing mental processing to slow down. The old saying that a cluttered house makes a cluttered mind is a proven scientific fact.

Dust and mold build up amongst clutter. When you have too many items in one area, cleaning becomes extremely difficult and it's easy to miss spots and overlook areas. A buildup of dust and mold can cause respiratory problems such as asthma and bronchitis.

Imagine there are two different offices. The first is stacked with books, paperwork, documents, and stationery. There is no room on any of the shelves, and you open a drawer that is crammed full of so much stuff you could hold a garage sale. No doubt there are plenty of interesting books to read and some nice pieces of stationary to work with, but the question is, can you find them when you need to? And if you really do need to look for them, how much time is it going to take? And how do you feel when you think you've found the book you were looking for, but as you go to grab it, the stack of papers resting on the books falls on your head? Or how do you feel when you know you left that luxury pen on the end of the desk but after moving a few items out of the way, you can't seem to find it?

Now, I want you to think about another office. When you walk in there is plenty of space for you to move around. Sure, the shelves have books on them, but they are organized like a library and there are only a few on each shelf. All the paperwork is in folders stored in filing cabinets, and all the stationary is neatly organized in pots and racks. Both offices are exactly the same size, have the same size desks, and the same number of shelves. The only difference between them is the number of items inside the office. The exact same office that just appears completely hopeless and unmanageable can be made to look simple and organized just by getting rid of some of the items. You will find that organization is possible when you throw away what you don't need.

According to the *United States News and World Report*, the average American spends approximately 12 months within the span of their life looking for lost items. Now just think about what you could do with an additional year added to your life. Think about how many extra things you could get done, the business you want to start, the weight you want to lose, the book you want to write, the degree you want to get, or the countries you want to travel to. Instead, you spend an entire year, looking for your keys! How ridiculous does that sound?

Research has discovered that the average home in the United States contains 300,000 items! In saying that, we don't use 80% of what we own! I am trying to get you to understand that the little bit of time you waste every day looking for those items because you have so much clutter and are so disorganized can quickly add up and cause you to miss some major opportunities.

According to the National Association of Professional Organizers, we receive an estimated 49,060 pieces of mail in a lifetime and almost half of it is junk mail. Every year, 16.6 billion catalogs are delivered to 100 million households. These catalogs are then stacked in a pile and left to collect dust, so they simply become more items adding to the clutter in your home.

Research also suggests that getting organized is on the list of top five New Year's resolutions, but only 20% of people get around to actually doing it. So if the majority of people have clutter in their homes, what's the point in me being any different? Here's why:

You Will Stop Losing Things

When was the last time you lost your cell phone or keys? On average, we spend approximately six minutes per day looking for our car keys in the morning. The top five items men are continuously looking for in their homes are the remote control, clean socks, the wedding album, driver's license, and car keys. This list is slightly different for women, which includes lipstick, the remote control, shoes, a child's toy, and wallet.

When your home is tidy and well organized, each item will have its own special place, and when you need it, you will know where to look for it. You will go directly to the filing cabinet for your insurance documents, the key hook on the walls for your car keys, the closet for your jacket, or the top shelf for the remote control. When everything is in order and in its rightful place, you will feel an overwhelming sense of peace.

YOU WILL SAVE MONEY

When was the last time you lost something, went out and bought it only to find the thing that you thought you had lost? Glue, batteries, socks, pens, light bulbs, etc. When your house is organized, you will know exactly where everything is, and you won't need to keep buying things you already own. According to the *Wall Street Journal,* a business adds 20% to their annual budgeting costs when they duplicate or purchase last-minute items. You waste a significant amount of money each time you run to the store to buy batteries that are probably stuck in the bottom of a drawer somewhere. By getting organized, you might even find yourself some lost coupons and save yourself even more money. People also waste money when they can't find their bills and end up paying them late. Statistics show that 23% of adults end up paying late fees, not because they couldn't afford to pay the bill but because they lost the bill!

Disorganization burns holes in your pockets. When you are clutter-free and organized, you won't need to rent a storage facility to house all the belongings that you don't actually need because you won't have any excess items to store! The clever people are making money out of your disorganization—storage facilities have become a $154 billion industry. Statistics state that one in eleven Americans at any one time are renting a unit, spending an estimated $1,000 every year to store things they don't need! Again, how ridiculous does that sound? As well as saving yourself a few dollars, you can also earn some money by selling the things you don't need.

CREATIVITY WILL FLOW

Having an organized environment frees your mind to become more relaxed and focused. When your surroundings are orderly, your brain is not forced to work so hard. On the other hand, when your environment is disorganized and full of clutter, there is no room in your brain to think straight, because whether you realize it or not, your mind is focused more on the mess than on being creative and developing new ideas. Clutter affects your ability to be at your best, it destroys your concentration, and pulls your attention away from the things that are the most important. When there is disorder in your environment, you will always have that nagging feeling of the things that you have left undone instead of giving your undivided attention to doing what you really want to do.

YOU WILL HAVE LESS STRESS IN YOUR LIFE

You probably haven't connected the dots, but I guarantee you that the majority of stress in your life is related to your disorganized space and messy environment. According to the Centers for Disease Control, the majority of our medical bills are due to stress-related conditions. Your surroundings dictate your mood, and one of the most therapeutic life-changing things you can do is get organized!

Ninety percent of people in the United States claim that a disorganized home or work environment has a negative effect on their overall well-being. Sixty-five percent say that mess has a negative effect on their mental health. Forty-three percent say that it demotivates them, which then leads to them feeling depressed.

When you know where things are, you feel a sense of calm. Imagine how less complicated your life would be if you could find everything you needed at the right time. In fact, studies have found that there is a direct link between anxiety, depression, and clutter. Misplacing items, being late, missing appointments, and untidy rooms all play a huge role in stress and anxiety, all of which are the result of being disorganized.

Experts in the field of organization have even stated that their clients have ended bad relationships, quit jobs they were not happy in, lost weight, and replaced bad habits with good ones after decluttering their homes. Clearing your space enables you to see things clearly.

YOU'LL BE MORE MOTIVATED TO ACHIEVE YOUR DREAMS

As you have just read, mess demotivates people, and when your home is disorganized and untidy, it's hard to see past the mess and focus on what's really important. When everything is organized, things get done on time, which means you have more hours in the day to work on the goals that you want to achieve.

YOU WILL SET THE STANDARDS FOR YOUR FAMILY

Children are products of their environment—if you are sloppy, they are going to be sloppy. How can you ask your kids to keep their rooms tidy when the rest of the house is a mess? It doesn't make any logical sense. If you want your children to respect and obey you, it is very important that you are living the life that you want them to live. Parents will often attempt to instill certain values and ideals into their children, but they have yet to master those values and ideals. My father was like this. He was always telling us off for leaving things unfinished; however, as I grew older, I realized that we had acquired one of his bad habits—he would always start projects and never finish them. He knew that it was a bad habit, and I'm sure it didn't make him feel very good about himself, so instead of working to change it, he attempted to enforce it on us. It didn't work because subconsciously, we had learned that leaving projects undone was the norm. I had to make a conscious decision to break this habit, but it took me many years to do so.

It is essential that you set a good example for your children to follow so that when they grow older, they will not depart from what you have taught them. As well as setting a good example, it's not good for small children, especially babies, to crawl around clutter; in fact, it can be extremely dangerous.

You Will Sleep Better

Everyone loves a good night's rest; however, if the room that you spend the majority of your time is in disarray, sleep will evade you. The bedroom is designed for rest, and studies have found that people with clutter in the bedroom experience more disturbances while asleep. There is nothing more frustrating than staring at a pile of junk before you close your eyes. When the last thing you see before you close your eyes and turn off the light is a mess, then that's the first thing you see when you open your eyes. You are programming your mind to accept that chaos is the norm. And whether you realize it or not, it places an imprint on your subconscious mind and interrupts your sleep at night. When you climb into a bed with clean sheets and a tidy room, you experience the peace and harmony required to enable you to get a good night's sleep.

Your Relationships Will Improve

What do your friends know you for? Is it the one who is always late because they got stuck in traffic or couldn't find their keys? The one who no one likes going to their house because it always smells of cat pee? They might make a joke of it, but are these really characteristics that you want to be known for? The NAPO conducted a survey of 1,397 people and asked them how much time it would take to get their house ready for a dinner party. Ten percent of respondents said they would never invite anyone to their home for dinner because it was so untidy, and six percent said that their homes were so untidy that it would take more than 40 hours to get it ready! These statistics sound absolutely outrageous, but they are a reality for a lot of people.

What happens when someone shows up at your house unexpectantly? Or when there is a medical emergency and the paramedics need to come inside your house? You won't have the time to get things in order. If you feel embarrassed about the state of your home, it's time to get it cleaned up so that you can invite more people over and spend time with the people you love.

Your house doesn't need to look like a show home. Even if you live in a trailer, a neat and orderly environment makes for a pleasant experience when people come over to visit. My motto in life is to be ready for anything, you never know what's going to happen or who is going to turn up at your door.

There are so many more benefits to being organized but space won't allow me to write about all of them. However, I'm sure you get the message that happiness and peace of mind can be as simple as getting your house in order.

CHAPTER 4:

DECLUTTERING AND UNEXPECTED TRANSFORMATION

My parents were far from wealthy. I was raised in government housing that only had two bedrooms to shelter 8 people! Life was not easy, but we managed. Not surprisingly, the house was always a mess—with eight children in two rooms, that shouldn't come as much of a shock. All my clothes were second hand; I don't remember ever getting anything new. My father worked out of town most of the time, so it was just my mom and us children, and in between taking care of us and making sure we had food to eat and clean clothes to wear, she didn't have time for much else.

However, my mom was a very gifted cake maker. When we could afford to, she would make the most delicious cakes—not only were they tasty, they were also pretty because she could do things with icing that I had never seen before. Even though we were happy, my parents wanted more, they just didn't know how to get it. To cut a long story short, my mom went to a conference with a friend one day and one of the main lessons she learned from it was about the importance of organization. I was pretty young when the change started, but all I remember was that one day I woke up and the kitchen was clean. You see, she would always leave the dishes overnight and get them done throughout the day. From that day forward, I never came downstairs in the morning to an untidy kitchen.

Then she started waking up earlier and cleaning the house. Although we only had two rooms, she made sure everything was neat and organized. She created a space for each of us to keep our belongings. She threw things out, scrubbed the carpet, cleaned the windows, the walls, the car. By the time she had finished, the house looked brand new. Now that the house was in order and she had a regular routine going to make sure that it was kept that way, she had extra time on her hands, so she started to make more cakes. While we were at school, she would walk around the neighborhood and sell them. We suddenly had extra money. My mom was a master at her craft, and word soon got around about her cakes, and the next thing I knew, she had set up shop from the house. People would come from all over the place to buy my mom's cakes! Within two years we had enough money to buy a bigger house, my dad quit his job, they opened a shop, they became millionaires, and the rest is history.

The moral of the story is that order breeds success. When my mom started doing the dishes at night instead of leaving them until the morning, she had no idea it would lead to a multimillion-dollar business, but what it did do was motivate her to get the rest of the house organized, and then she realized that she had all this free time on her hands. You will never move to the next phase in your life until you can take care of the basics.

All my friends and family know that I have a passion for teaching about vision. The popular school of thought is that if you can see it in your mind's eye, you can believe it and achieve it. Nice principle, but there is more to it than that. I strongly believe there is a missing piece of the puzzle that success gurus are failing to teach—the universe/God/your personal higher power must be able to trust you before it will give you what you want. So anytime any of my friends are having difficulty accomplishing their goals, they will ask me where I think they are going wrong, and it is always something really simple.

Some friends of mine—let's call them the Smiths—were struggling financially, but they desperately needed a new car and they decided to dream big about it. The Smiths wanted a brand-new Honda Civic paid for in cash. They spoke affirmations over their dreams and goals, they had all types of side hustles going on, but nothing seemed to be working out. When they approached me about this, I asked them to take a look at their current car. Now, I had never paid it any attention prior to this, but when I did, I realized that the state of their old car was what was blocking them from getting a new one. It was an absolute mess, despicable to look at on the inside and out. People were so horrified with the dirt that they had used their fingers to carve out the words "PLEASE CLEAN ME I DON'T LIKE BEING DIRTY" across the side of the car!

So, I let the Smiths know that they were not going to get the car they were dreaming about until they cleaned up the car they were driving. I told them to act as if the car that they were driving was their new car to show their higher power that they could be trusted with the vehicle they wanted. If not, when they got their brand-new Honda Civic, it would end up looking like the same piece of junk they are driving now. Well, they took my advice and cleaned up the car and kept it clean. Within three months, they had a brand-new Honda Civic, just as they had dreamed!

The bottom line is that you are not going to get what you want until you can be faithful with what you've got. If you want a new house, job, or car, one of the most powerful strategies for success is to live as if you've already got what you want, put excellence into practice as you make your way to your desired destination. As a rule of thumb, if there is anything in your environment that you can't look at and say, "This is excellent," then fix it until it is excellent!

A Character of Excellence Opens the Door to Success

We live in a world where everything is given to us immediately. We make microwave meals or grab a hamburger from a fast food restaurant instead of cooking, we get liposuction instead of working out, we buy things on credit instead of saving for it, and the list is endless. Society has trained us to grab and go, so we have no patience to put the effort into what we really want. We go to school and are told to focus on choosing the right career path, but whatever happened to focusing on choosing the right character path? Today, it is rare to find qualities such as perseverance, determination, and attention to detail in a person. Whether it's at home or at work, we think we can get away with doing the bare minimum, but at the same time expect to see huge results. I am sorry to disappoint you, but life doesn't work like that. When you are faithful with the little that you have, and that means doing things like putting your best efforts forward even when you are working in a job that you hate, you will strategically place yourself on the pathway to success.

For example, if you are currently renting but want to own your own home, treat the rented accommodation as if it were the mansion you want to own. Don't leave the carpets stained because you know they don't belong to you, don't bang holes into the walls to hang your pictures up unless you are planning on fixing them before you leave. If you can't be trusted with someone else's property, why should you be trusted with your own?

So, to conclude this chapter, my personal lesson in success is to treasure what you have and finish what you start. It is essential that you take care of the small things you own if you want to acquire more, but it is equally as important to finish what you start. When projects are left incomplete, no matter how small, they take up both physical and mental space. When you have that irritating feeling that you need to finish painting that room, clean out the attic, donate those old clothes to charity, or pay the rest of those bills, they occupy mental space simply because they are not finished.

There is more to this than not finishing things around the house, it also extends to the things you should be doing in life such as opening a savings account, getting into shape, or finishing an online course. Whatever it is, unfinished projects steal your peace and drain your energy. When you procrastinate in the areas of life that might not seem important, you carry that same attitude into the important areas of your life.

CHAPTER 5:

CREATING A SENSE OF ORDER

Walking into a clutter-free, pristine, and stream-lined room is a wonderful feeling! However, for the majority of people, this doesn't come naturally, but this doesn't mean you can't learn to create this sense of order. When it comes to organizing your home, the goal is to make it functional so that everyone knows where everything is at any given time. This is what will create the peaceful environment you are looking for.

Your aim should be to do everything with excellence, and that includes washing the dishes before you go to bed, making sure your car is in the best condition, and making your bed first thing in the morning. Whatever you do, no matter how small, do it to the best of your ability and you will begin to feel a sense of pride for yourself and your surroundings. So, let's get started with organizing your life!

Take Photos: You want to take photos so that you have something to remind you of where you don't want to go back to and to remind you of how far you've come.

Staying Motivated: One of the hardest things about getting your life in order is not the process but staying motivated. The bottom line is that no one wants to work hard; we want the easy way out. Most people would much rather spend their time watching soap operas on the couch eating milk and cookies, but that's not going to get you anywhere is it? During my organizing phase, I listened to motivational music and teachings by powerful public speakers such as Les Brown, Tony Robbins and Brian Tracy. Not only was I getting my life in order, but I was also learning some life-changing messages. I found that if I ever tried to get anything done without listening to something motivational, I was not as productive.

Set an Alarm: It's impossible for you to work all day without having a break. I used a tool called the Pomodoro method, in which you basically work for 25 minutes and then have a five-minute break. Do this four times, have a 10-minute break, and then go back to five-minute breaks. Repeat until the end of the day. The website I used was www.tomato-timer.com/. Together with the motivational music and teachings, this timer really helps you to focus, it's almost as if you are racing against time because you know you only have a short window to get something done before the timer goes off.

CREATIVE IDEAS FOR ORGANIZING
THE FOYER, THE BACKDOOR, OR THE ENTRYWAY

Anyone that comes into your home will pass through one of these areas first, which is why it's so important for them to be free of clutter. Imagine someone walking into your home for the first time and the first thing they are introduced to is a pile of mess! Not only is it embarrassing for you, but a messy home makes guests feel uncomfortable. I know what I'm like when I walk into an untidy house, I don't want to sit down in case I leave with my trousers a different color and neither do I want a drink in case I swallow a roach! Here are some ideas to organize these areas:

- Shoes, Baseball Caps, Umbrellas, etc.: Perhaps after you get rid of all those books you will have an empty bookshelf. Turn it into storage space and use it to house the random items that are usually left around the doorway.

- Coats, Car Keys, House Keys, Dog Leashes, Backpacks, etc.: Fix a few hooks to the backdoor and use them to hang up these items. Make it a rule that as soon as anyone enters the house, the first thing they must do is hang their belongings on one of these hooks.

- Gloves, Scarves, Newspapers, Sports Equipment, etc.: Baskets and bins are relatively cheap, so they won't break the bank. Give one to each family member and put their name on it. They are to put all their belongings into the bin when they return home. However, make sure that these bins and baskets are monitored because they've got overload potential. You don't want anything and everything stored in them; they are only for certain items. Make sure you are very specific about this.

Additional Tip: Some entryways have the potential to look quite solemn and uninviting. You know, the type of hallways that are so dark and gloomy that you are scared to get to the end of it because you don't know what's waiting at the other side! You can brighten it up by hanging a mirror on the wall or painting the area a light and fluffy color.

THE LIVING ROOM

Have you ever wondered why the living room is called the living room? It's because that's where we spend most of our time when we are in the house, so it would only make sense that it is well organized. It can be pretty easy to get this room organized.

- Games, Blankets, Pillows: People usually stuff these items behind the couch or have them piled up against a wall. Buy some storage bins and stash these items away.

- Remote Controls, Newspapers, Magazines: Do you have any shelves in your living room? If not, get some and use them to house these items.

- Cords and Phone Chargers: The living room floor is often overrun with cords and phone chargers. If you have a drawer attached to your coffee table, fold up your cords and tuck them into empty toilet rolls, you can then tuck them away neatly into a drawer.

THE BEDROOMS

Bedrooms can get very untidy because this is where we keep our clothes, shoes, belts, makeup, etc. Keep these rooms organized by doing the following.

Bed Linens: When you don't have any storage space, bed linens are left wherever they will fit. If you have an old dresser, before you throw it out, remove the drawers and use them to house bed linens. You can then slide the drawers neatly under the bed.

Writing Supplies, Books, Journals: Most people have a terrible habit of allowing these items to pile up around their bed. If you have a bedside table with a drawer, use the drawer to store these items instead of leaving them on the floor.

Decorative Pieces, Frames: Make use of your wall space and hang these items up. All you need to do is bang a few nails into the wall.

Work Supplies, Magazines: Purchase an ottoman and put it at the foot of your bed, you can use it to store these items.

Dirty Clothes: Are you guilty of allowing your dirty clothes to pile up on the floor behind the door? Not to worry, I was too! Use the space available on the back of your door to hang a laundry hamper that you can put your dirty clothes in.

Arranging Your Clothes: Before I started to get my life in order, my clothes were stuffed wherever they could fit. And when I needed to wear anything, I would pull everything out to find what I was looking for. I was constantly surrounded by piles of clothes until I learned how to fold and organize them properly.

Folding Button-Down Shirts

- Lay the shirt down on a flat surface (a bed or an ironing board will do)
- Button the shirt from the top down, but leave the cuffs open
- Turn the shirt over and stretch the arms out to the sides
- Fold one arm over so that the shirt is folded in half
- Fold the same arm at an angle back on itself
- Do the same to the other side

How to Fold a Sweater

- Lay the sweater face up on a flat surface
- Use your hands to smooth out any wrinkles

- Fold the sleeves across the front of the sweater so they end up touching the base of the sweater
- Take the bottom of the sweater and fold it up towards the neck

How to Fold a T-Shirt

- Lay the t-shirt out on a flat surface
- Use your hands to smooth out any wrinkles
- Fold the t-shirt in half long ways
- Fold the sleeves backward and smooth them over
- Take the bottom of the t-shirt and fold it up to the end of the sleeves
- Fold the collar down on top of the sleeves

How to Fold Jeans

- Put your hand into each pocket and make sure they are pushed down
- Hold the jeans at the waist and shake them out
- Lay them out onto a flat surface
- Fold one leg on top of the other and use your hands to smooth out any wrinkles
- Make sure both legs are perfectly lined up
- Pick the legs up from the bottom and fold them up to the waist
- Fold the jeans again by doing the same

How to Fold a Skirt

- If the skirt has pockets, use your hands to make sure the pockets are pushed down

- Lay the skirt on a flat surface and smooth out any wrinkles
- Fold the bottom of the skirt up towards the waist
- Fold the skirt again corner to corner
- Do this one more time depending on the size of the skirt

HOW TO ORGANIZE YOUR CLOSET

Before you start organizing your closet, the first thing you need to do is go through your clothes and get rid of anything you don't wear. If you haven't worn an item of clothing in a year or more, you don't wear it! You can either donate them, sell them, or give them to a friend. Whatever you do, just get rid of them!

Storage baskets: If there is anything you can't store away neatly, put them into a storage basket. If you don't have any, they are pretty cheap to buy.

Use all Available Space: If you have a spare wall in your closet, fix a towel bar to it, and hang your scarves and belts on it.

Use a Boot Organizer: Boots can be difficult in a closet. They fall over at the slightest touch and, eventually, you just get fed up and leave them on the floor. A boot organizer hangs from the clothes rack and each boot is attached to its own clip.

Add Your Dressing Table: If you have enough space, you can create more room in your bedroom by putting your dresser and mirror in the closet.

Arrange Shoes on the Door: This idea only works for heels—screw towel rails on the back of the door and hang your shoes on them.

Use Shelf Dividers: Instead of lumping everything together on the top shelf, use shelf dividers to separate your folded clothes.

Add Another Bar: Once you've gotten rid of the clothes you don't wear, and you still don't have enough room, double up your space by adding another bar in the closet.

Use Good Hangers: If you use those old wire hangers, it's time to get rid of them, they make your closet look unkempt. Buy metal slim open hangers, not only are they sturdy and look better, they make it easier to get your clothes off the rack.

A Higher Rod: If you don't have enough space in your closet for two rods, hang the one that you've got higher up. This will create more space for you to put something underneath, like a shoe rack or a dresser.

Hats, Socks, Gloves, etc.: These small items can become overwhelming when you have too many of them. Fruit baskets are great for putting these items in and using vertical space.
Sweaters: Sweaters are so big and bulky that they just take up too much space; get them out of the way by rolling them up and slotting them into the cubbies of a hanging shoe organizer.

Scarves: Take a single hanger and attach shower hooks to it and then neatly hang your scarves over them.

Underwear: Prevent your underwear from getting lost in the back of the drawer by storing them in shoeboxes.

Purses: Hang wire baskets fastened to the back of the closet door. Command hooks are a good way to store purses, handbags, and other accessories.

THE BATHROOM

This is another room in the house where guests will definitely visit, so it is essential to keep it well organized at all times. Also, you will find that it is easier to get ready in the mornings when the bathroom is tidy.

- Hair ties, Brushes, and Combs: Most people have drawers in their bathroom, and they just stuff things in there, which means they have to rummage through a pile of junk to get to anything. Keep the drawer organized by putting a kitchen utensil tray in it and arranging these items in each compartment.

- Hair Tools: Store items such as flat irons, curling irons, and blow driers in a magazine holder.

- Nail Polish: You can either purchase a nail polish shelf or store your nail polish collection in cookie jars, depending on how many you have. You can separate them into colors in different jars. If you really want to get creative, you can use a spice rack.

- Bobby Pins: The next time you buy a packet of Tic Tac's, don't throw away the empty container, use them to store your bobby pins.

- Lipstick: Instead of piling your lipsticks up in a bathroom drawer, arrange them in miniature loaf or muffin pans.

- Makeup: Ok, so I know I have spent the majority of this book telling you to get rid of stuff, but there are a few things that can come in handy for storage such as your daughter's old bead organizer. They have great compartments for women to fit all their make up in. If not, purchase a makeup stand from your local supermarket.

- Perfumes: Save some space in your bathroom by using a 2-tiered cake tray to show off your perfume collection.

- Cleaning Products: Instead of leaving them on the floor around the toilet, put your cleaning products into a bucket and store them under the sink.

- Medicine: All family members should know where the medicine cabinet is. It should be stored in one location in the bathroom instead of multiple different places, which is usually the case. You can attach small storage bins to the inside of your cabinet door and arrange the medicine in them.

- Towels: Organize your towels by size, sets, and color. Fold them neatly and arrange them in drawers, storage boxes, or on shelves.

- Vanity: Your countertop should be as empty as possible. Not only does this look neater, but it also makes it easier to clean. If you have run out of drawer and cabinet space, make sure you display the nicest items on your countertops.

JEWELRY

- Necklaces: Eliminate messy piles of necklaces by hanging them individually onto a pegboard.

- Bracelets: Neatly stack bracelets onto a paper towel holder.

- Earrings: Stop your small earrings from getting lost and mixed up by arranging them in an ice cube tray.

THE KITCHEN

- Produce: Once again, this is where some of your old items come in handy. Hang an old shower caddy on the inside of the pantry door or on the side of the cabinet to store things like peppers and onions.

- Soup Cans: Wire baskets are great for stacking soup or any other type of cans. They allow you to keep the labels visible and they make cans easier to stack.

- Cutting Boards: Wire bins come in very handy when it comes to storing cutting boards. Attach one to the back of the cabinet door.

- Long Handled Utensils: If you have an old flower vase, use it to store your tall utensils in and arrange it on top of the counter.

- Boxed Goods: You can cut down on storage space in the pantry by using clear canisters and emptying your boxed goods such as cereal and rice into them.

- Plastic Wrap, Tin Foil, and Sandwich Bags: A cardboard magazine holder is excellent for storing these items. They keep them organized and make them easy to grab hold of when needed.

- Tea Bags: Tea bags should be kept in a closed container to keep them fresh. Store them in see-through mason jars with airtight lids.

- Plastic Tupperware Lids: Are you forever buying new Tupperware because you are always losing the lids? Store them in a metal cooling rack attached to a basket to keep them from growing legs and going on the run.

- Cleaning Products: Free up some space on your cabinet floor by hanging your cleaning products on a tension rod under the sink.

Oven Drawers: Do me a favor, go and open your oven drawer. I guarantee you will find nothing in there that's oven related. We toss everything in there to keep the area free from clutter, but then we end up making an even bigger mess; but because we can't see it, we think it's ok.

It's not a big drawer; actually, its most likely the smallest drawer in the kitchen, neither is it easy to access. This is one of the reasons you tend to throw everything in there, you don't think anyone will ever see it. However, there is the proper use for everything in the kitchen, and that includes the oven drawer. If you can manage it, the best way to declutter an oven drawer is to keep it empty. If not, keep it to these items only:

- Flat items: Store flat items such as baking pans and lids in one half of the oven drawer. Don't keep them in the middle or you will make a mess when looking for other items.

- Lids: In general, pots are stackable, which means you are left with finding somewhere to put the lids. Store them in the oven drawer for easy access.

The Plastic Bag Issue: Plastic bags can become a real problem. Most of us go grocery shopping on a weekly basis, and instead of recycling bags, we tend to accumulate more every week! To eliminate this problem, put the majority of your plastic bags in the recycling bin. Keep 5 large bags and 10 small bags, then store them somewhere you will have easy access to them.

- Old milk carton: Cut the top off a milk carton and wash it out. Stuff the plastic bags in them and store them in the cupboard under the sink or in a place that's convenient for you.

- An empty tissue box: An empty tissue box is ready to use. Place the plastic bags inside the box and store them in the cupboard under the sink or in a place that's convenient for you.

- A pantyhose leg: Cut the leg off one of your old pantyhose, stuff the plastic bags inside, and hang it up inside a cupboard, in the pantry, or a place that's convenient for you.

Sink and Dish Area: It's easy for this area to become cluttered, kids leave their dishes in the sink, and before you know it, there's a big mess. You can avoid this by doing the following:

- If you have a dishwasher, make sure the dishes are stacked here instead of left on the sides or in the sink.

- If you don't have a dishwasher, leave a dish rack in the sink. When it gets full, you will know it's time to get your rubber gloves on and do some washing up.

THE LAUNDRY ROOM

Laundry rooms are typically pretty small, and with limited space you want to make sure the space that you do have is well utilized.

- Bleach, Dryer Sheets, Detergent: If you don't have cabinets in your laundry room, a hanging storage rack is a great option. You can also install shelves above the washer and dryer to store your supplies. The back of the door is often an overlooked storage space, you can hang a shoe organizer over it and use it to store your appliances.
- The Ironing Board: Hide the ironing board by hanging it on coat hooks behind the door.

THE PLAY ROOM

Kids love their playroom, and they also know how to keep it looking a hot mess! Get your children's playroom organized by doing the following:

- Toys: There is not really much point in organizing toys because they are going to get messed up quickly. Before your kids start playing, lay a blanket on the floor and dump the toys on top. When they have finished playing, pull the blanket together and put the toys back into the storage bin.

- Dolls: Hang a shoe organizer over the back of the door and store all dolls, action figures, and barbies.

- Puzzles: Empty puzzle pieces into Ziplock bags and throw the boxes away.

- Stuffed Animals: Hang a hammock or a plastic chain from the ceiling and attach all your child's stuffed animals.

- Board Games: If you don't have any already, install shelves to the walls and place all board games on them.

- Books: Does your child have an old wagon? Use it to store all their storytime books.

THE OFFICE

Not every home has an office; but if you do, this is how to keep it organized:

Files: Get rid of all your manila folders and replace them with color-coded ones. This will allow you to immediately find what you need. To get used to the system, you might want to write a list and stick it to the wall. For example: Green = Bills, Blue = Insurance, etc.

Desk Essentials: The spice rack has so many different uses and one of them is to store your office supplies. Use spice containers to house post-it notes, rubber bands, thumb tacks, paper clips, etc.

THE GARAGE

Think about this for a minute: the random items taking up so much space in your garage are worth very little in comparison to the expensive car that's sitting in the driveway! Is that not incentive enough to get your garage in order?

- Beach Balls, Soccer Balls, Basket Balls: Corral these items against the wall with bungee cords.

- Miscellaneous Items: Garages are full of random items, such as tacks, nails, pins, and rubber bands. Get them out the way by storing them in a muffin pan; the small compartments will allow you to easily store these items.

- Nuts and Bolts: A great way to get those nuts and bolts out the way is to store them in a spice rack.

- Tools: Attach a towel bar to the wall and then attach hooks to them, you can then hang tools such as garden hoses and rakes and spades.

THE CAR

Most people never think about getting their car in order because they don't spend a lot of time in it. Here is how you can make it a bit more organized.

- Tissues, Snacks, Hand Sanitizers: A great way to store these items is to drape mesh or plastic shower pockets over the back of the front car seats. This gives the kids easy access to these things, and they can put them back when they're finished instead of leaving them on the floor.

- Cups, Toys: A plastic caddy is great for storing miscellaneous items during your journey.

That's pretty much it guys. You don't need to utilize all the suggestions but pick the ones that are best suited to your living space. Remember, organization and cleanliness keeps you focused, your mind clear, your concentration sharp, and most of all, it makes you feel good. It's going to take a while to get all this done, but once it's complete, you will feel on top of the world.

CHAPTER 6:

30 DAY KNOCK OUT CHALLENGE

I think you've read enough now, it's time to get moving! By now, I hope you know what you need to do to get your life organized. In what areas do you feel as if your life is spiraling out of control? Take a look at your surroundings, what does your clutter say about you? Where are you taking on too much? Why do you think you have accumulated the number of things that you have? Thinking about this stuff is overwhelming, I know, I have been there; however, this step is essential if you are going to move forward.

It is in no way going to take you 30 days to declutter your home, but the aim is to get things done in 30-day increments.

Step 1: Planning is an important part of life—if you don't know where you are going, how are you going to get there? A plan is like a detailed roadmap that tells you how to get to your destination. Decide where you are going to start first. I chose the messiest room in the house. I thought if I can get that done then I can do anything, and I was certainly right.

Step 2: Write down a list of the top 10 things that need to be done in the room that you have been putting off. For example, folding the laundry, getting the bills in order, etc.

Step 3: Now attack this list with a 30-day knockout challenge! Get your calendar and block out the next 30 days with everything that you need to do. So, for example, July 1 might say: Organize shoes, fold clothes. Make up your mind to ensure that everything you include on this list is completed within the 30 days. As you get through with each one, tick them off as you go along. Believe me when I say you will be absolutely fired up and motivated once you get to the end of the 30 days. You will realize that you have completed everything you set out to. You will want to kick yourself for taking so long in the first place, which will give you the drive, motivation, and the confidence to achieve bigger goals.

As you begin to transform your home and live a life of excellence in every area, it will show, and people will start to notice, admire, and respect you. Instead of feeling drained from the mess you were forced to look at every day, you will feel energetic, enthusiastic, and excited about life. No longer will you be controlled by your circumstances, but you will have full control over them, and you will start to run towards the destiny that you know you deserve.

Don't let the miniscule things in your life drown out the things that are the most important. Develop a mental attitude that is determined to get things done no matter how large or small.

Turn Your Trash into Cash

As you have read, excess items in the home are a waste of money. The good news is that it's not all doom and gloom; you can turn some of your trash into cash. Remember that one man's trash is another man's treasure! What you don't use someone else will.

A recent survey found that over half of the employees who participated said that saving more money was on the top of the list for their New Year resolution; however, less than 69% of Americans have $1,000 in savings. You have also read that Americans love to waste money storing items they don't need, contributing to the multi-billion dollar per year storage industry. If you are guilty of owning a storage unit, go empty it right now!

eBay conducted a survey and found that the average household stores over 50 unused items worth approximately $3,100. Just think about what you could do with that extra money! Once you have decided what you are going to throw away and what you are going to keep, set another 30-day challenge to sell the items. Whatever you can't sell, donate. The idea here is to get the things that you don't need out of your house and into the hands of the people that do need them.

Decide how much money you want to make from your items, and make sure you stick to it. You see, once you get your stuff online and you open the door for people to contact you, there are going to be people who will want to trade stuff. In other words, instead of paying for it, they will want to give you something else that is of the same value. Do not get sucked into this game because some of these deals can be quite tempting. Remember, your aim is to make money from the items you want to get rid of, not gain more items. Think about what you will be able to do with the money: pay off credit card bills, pay down a car note, or put the money into savings.

It is also important to mention that the decluttering process is not just about getting rid of things you don't want, it's also about getting rid of the things you don't use—you know, all those items that are lurking in the back of the closet that you fantasize about using one day! A rule of thumb to go by is to get rid of anything that hasn't been used in 12 months or more.

How to Turn Your Trash into Cash

You are probably thinking, "Well this sounds like a great idea, but how do I go about doing it?" Not to worry, I'm about to show you how.

Selling Tips

Selling your unused and unwanted items is a great idea, but you need to know what you are doing before you start. Here are a few tips to get you started:

Do Some Research: If you've got some expensive pieces like electronic goods, go online and find out how much they are selling brand new and then price them at slightly cheaper. For example, if you have a phone that's worth $350, sell it for $275. You are selling the items cheaper than they are worth because, even though you may not have used them, they are considered second hand. You also want to give buyers an incentive to purchase from you. You can also check sites like eBay and Amazon to find out the going rates for your items.

Descriptions: If you choose to sell your items online, it is essential that you give an accurate description of the product. If the speaker has scratches on it, let potential buyers know. At the end of the day, if you are not honest about the condition, the buyer has the right to return it and request a refund. You can avoid this by being upfront from the start. You also want to make sure that you take good pictures of the items against a clear background. For example, if you are selling a black phone, photograph it against a white background.

Prime Time Posting: According to research, the best time to list items on an auction site is between the hours of 7:00 pm to 9:00 pm (CST). However, the times might be different for your local area, so do some research before posting.

THE BEST ITEMS TO SELL

There are certain items that are in higher demand than others; for example, you might not get very far trying to sell a box of paperclips, but clothing and electronics will sell better. Here are some of the most popular items to sell:

Books: How many novels and textbooks do you have that you no longer read. Instead of them collecting dust, sell them and collect some cash. www.bookriot.com will give you a list of the best sites to sell books, or you can sell them to your local bookstore.

CDs and DVDs: CDs and DVDs are a thing of the past; most people have an ancient pile stacked up in the corner of their living room. You can sell your CDs and DVDs on websites such as www.ziffit.com.

Gift Cards: They sound like an odd thing to sell, but they sell; you might have been given some gift cards as a gift, but you haven't used them and don't intend to. Studies have found that approximately $750 million in gift cards a year are never redeemed! That's a lot, but I'm guilty of doing the same. Consider selling your gift cards for cash, especially when it's a gift card from a store you are not particularly fond of. You can get some decent money for your gift cards or you can exchange them for cash on sites such as www.cardcash.com/sell-gift-cards/ and www.cardpool.com.

Clothes: You don't need a closet full of designer clothes to be able to sell them. You will be surprised at what people will buy at a discounted price. You can sell the clothes you no longer wear on sites like www.amazon.com, www.eBay.com, and www.etsy.com.

Furniture: The best places to sell your furniture are antique malls, consignment shops, and a garage sale.

Electronics: www.yourenew.com, www.buybackworld.com, www.gazelle.com, and www.usell.com are just a few sites that will buy your electronic goods for cash. These include desktop computers, phones, digital cameras, laptops, iPods, and much more.

Refrigerators and Air Conditioning Units: How many of you have an old refrigerator or air conditioning unit collecting cobwebs in the back of the shed? Well did you know that your local energy company will take these items off your hands at no cost to you and give you cash for them in return?

Musical Instruments: My kids wanted all sorts of music lessons when they were younger, but as they grew into their teenage years they were no longer interested, so we had a pile of musical instruments in the house. I am sure some of you can relate to this, it was a waste of money; some music stores and pawn shops will pay you decent money for your unwanted musical instruments.

Jewelry: Has your boyfriend just dumped you? Don't waste your time or energy mourning over the breakup, cash in on that ring, necklace, or bracelet he bought you. You can sell your jewelry on sites such as www.neverlikeditanyway.com and www.idonowidont.com. They will give you top dollar for them too!

Get Selling!

Now that you know what to sell, it's time to start selling! Here are some great ways to sell your unused items.

Garage Sale: Get a flyer made up, it doesn't need to be anything fancy, take some pictures of some of the best items you want to sell, paste them onto a word document and provide details of the garage sale, location, time, a list of the items, etc. Get the kid, (if you don't have any, do it yourself) and go around town handing out these fliers. Put them in letterboxes, leave them in stores, hairdressers, and pin them up on bus stop windows. The point is to let the entire town know that you are having a garage sale! You won't get the highest prices with a garage sale because people expect bargains, but it will help you to get rid of the majority of your stuff.

Pawn Shops: If you have a lot of old electronics and jewelry and you don't want to deal with the hassle of selling them yourself, take them to a pawn shop. They will gladly take them off your hands. Again, you won't get the highest prices because they have to sell them and make a profit, but you will get something.

The Internet: One of the main benefits of selling your items online is that you get to put them in front of a global audience which means you have a higher chance of selling them because more people will be scoping your stuff! The best sites to use are eBay.com, Amazon.com, Etsy.com, and a phone app called LetGo. LetGo is an app geared for local selling and buying. The plus side is you don't have to worry about shipping, and shipping costs, as people just come to pick up your stuff! Just make sure that you use discretion when selling to strangers, and meet in a public place when you're ready to sell. There are tons more, but these are the best. There is no complicated sign-up process, simply load up a picture and a description of the items you want to sell, sit back and wait for the bids to come rolling in!

Auctions: This is only for people who have some really rare and antique items; you won't get very far trying to sell the sewing machine you don't use at an auction. To find out how much your items might be worth, you can visit an online auction site or go to your local auction house if there is one in your area.

Consignment Shops: Do you have any designer clothes you don't wear? Or any expensive furniture? If so, take them to a consignment shop and they will gladly take them off your hands. There are also consignment shops that take toys, video games, children and baby clothes. Consignment shops basically sell your items for you, they sell them at the highest price possible and split the profits with you.

Social Media: If you don't want to sell your items to random people, advertise your things on your social media profiles and sell them to friends and family instead.

CHAPTER 7:

ENVIRONMENTALLY FRIENDLY CLEANING METHODS

Once you have gotten rid of what you don't need in each room, the next step is cleaning! Before you start rearranging things, you want to make sure that the area is clean. I am a huge fan of using natural products to clean. Not only are they better for your health, but they are also better for the environment. We have been fooled into believing that the only way to remove grime, grease, and dirt is by using harsh chemicals. This is so not true! I have been making my own natural cleaning products for years, and I can tell you that they work even better than the commercial stuff. I remember the last time I used store-bought cleaning products. I bent over the bathtub and started spraying what I was using at the time. I had to squint my eyes because I could feel the burn. I assumed this was normal, as I had been using these products for so many years, but something clicked at that moment and I just thought to myself, "There is no way this can be safe." My eyes were burning, my nose was running, and I was coughing—that's not healthy! So, I started looking into the negative effects of store-bought cleaning products and I was very disturbed at what I found. May

I add, I wasn't reading random blogs by people who have a love for the planet, what I found came from professional and credible sources. One of them was the Cancer Prevention Coalition (CPC). They have conducted several studies and found that the majority of American household cleaning products contain a high level of carcinogenic and toxic ingredients. It has also been found that most of these ingredients cause cancer!

- Lysol Disinfectant Spray is mixed with an ingredient called "orthophenylphenol" (OPP). Research has found that this product causes bladder tumors.
- Ajax Cleanser is made up of an ingredient called "crystalline silica," which causes skin, eye, and lung irritation.
- Ortho Weed Killer contains an ingredient called "Dichlopophenoxyacetate," which causes lymphoma, cancer, and soft tissue sarcoma.

After this shocking discovery, I started looking for alternatives, and my search led me to products that I could start using immediately because they were sitting in my cupboard! These included baking soda, lemon juice, and vinegar!

Here are some house cleaning tips using natural products that will turn your home into the palace it was destined to be!

CLEANING YOUR LIVING ROOM

Cleaning your sofa and cushions: Before you start, check the care tag to ensure that it has a "W" written on it. This means that you can self-clean your sofa without ruining it. If not, you will need to contact a professional to clean it for you.

- Fill a bucket with lukewarm water
- Add half a cup of white vinegar

- Add one spoon of baking powder
- Use a long wooden spoon to stir and combine
- Dip a sponge into the mixture and squeeze out the excess water
- Start cleaning the cushions first and rub the sponge over both sides
- Once clean, put them up against a wall to dry
- To keep them from touching, place clean towels or kitchen paper towels between them
- To clean the sofa, take it apart and use the same cleaning process for the cushions
- Let the sofa air dry
- Make sure the sofa and cushions are completely dry before putting them back together

How to Clean Leather Chairs

- Add 1/3 of white vinegar to a glass jar
- Add 2/3 of olive oil
- Put a lid on the jar and shake it vigorously to combine the ingredients
- Take a dry cloth and pour out some of the mixture onto it
- Use the cloth to buff the chairs

How to Get Rid of Pet Smells from Your Sofa

- Pull your sofa apart and air dry it outside for as long as possible. Use a carpet beater or a stick to beat out the salt residue remaining from urine
- Sprinkle a generous amount of baking soda over the couch parts and let it sit for the night
- Vacuum the sofa the next day

How to Clean Your Dining Room

The dining table is the most important part of the dining room. They come in a variety of materials, sizes, and shapes. Once damaged, they can be very expensive to repair, so here are some tips to restore and clean your dining table.

How to Disguise Scratches

- Select a nut that is the same or similar in color to your dining table—a walnut works well
- In a horizontal direction, rub the nut over the scratch
- Darken the scratch by dipping a cotton swab in iodine and going over the scratch
- You may need to repeat the above step several times to get the color to match

How to Remove Smudges

- Fill a large bowl with lukewarm water
- Add half a cup of white vinegar
- Soak a cotton cloth in the liquid squeeze out the excess
- Wipe over the area

How to Clean a Glass Table

- Add one tablespoon of white vinegar to a spray bottle
- Add one cup of water
- Add one cup of rubbing alcohol
- Shake the spray bottle vigorously
- Spray the glass table and use a lint-free cloth to wipe over it

HOW TO CLEAN THE BATHROOM

We use the bathroom daily, so it has the potential to get the dirtiest. Mildew, trapped hair in the drain, a smelly toilet, and whatever else you can think of makes it a very unpleasant place to clean, yet it has to be done. Not only do you visit the bathroom daily, but it is the one room that your guests are most likely to visit, so it's important to keep the bathroom clean at all times.

How to Clean the Inside of the Toilet

- In a large bowl, combine one tablespoon of baking soda with half a cup of white vinegar
- Pour this mixture into the toilet bowl making sure it goes around the sides
- Leave the mixture for 30 minutes
- Use a toilet brush to scrub the bowl
- Flush the toilet

How to Clean the Outside of the Toilet

- In a spray bottle mix one-part vinegar with three parts water and one part baking soda
- Give the bottle a good shake
- Spray the entire toilet bowl
- Let it sit for around 10 minutes
- Use a damp cloth to remove the dirt and the solution

How to Remove Limescale From the Toilet

If the limescale is above the waterline, gently scrape it off with a butter knife. If it is below the waterline, push the water down with a toilet brush and then scrape. If the limescale is on the base of the toilet bowl, you will need to remove the water with a cup before scraping. Once you have managed to get rid of the limescale, flush the toilet.

For really stubborn limescale, fill the toilet with half a gallon of vinegar and leave it overnight. In the morning use a toilet brush to scrub the bowl and then flush.

Cleaning Your Sink's Drain

- Wearing gloves, remove the covering and pull out any gunk and hair from the drain
- Pour 3/4 cup of baking soda down the sink hole
- Pour 1/2 a cup of white vinegar down the sink hole
- Use a stopper to block the drain for 30 minutes
- Boil some water, remove the stopper, and pour it down the drain

How to Clean the Toilet Waste Pipe

If you have never cleaned your toilet waste pipe, let me warn you, you are in for a nasty surprise!

- Soak a damp cloth in vinegar
- Use the cloth to scrub the pipe
- For difficult stains soak the cloth in vinegar and wrap it around the pipe and let it sit for 30 minutes before wiping

How to Remove Soap Scum

- Create a paste by combining baking soda and dish liquid
- Soak a sponge or a cloth in the mixture
- Scrub at the soap scum until it dissolves
- Soak a cloth in warm water and wipe the area clean

How to Remove Mold

- Pour white vinegar into a spray bottle
- Spray the mold and leave it to dry
- Spray the mold again and use a damp cloth to remove the mold

You might have to do this a few times to get rid of the mold. You can prevent the buildup of mold by spraying the bath or shower with a water and vinegar mix daily.

How to Clean the Shower Curtain

You can clean vinyl or plastic shower curtains in several ways. If the curtain is not too dirty, simply spray it with a combination of vinegar and water and then clean it with a damp cloth. For a more thorough clean, soak a sponge in water, sprinkle it with baking powder, and then give the curtain a good scrub. If you've neglected your shower curtain for a while and it's infested with mildew, you will need to take the curtain outside. Lay it on the ground and scrub it with baking soda and vinegar. If all else fails, put the curtain in the washing machine and add ½ a cup of baking soda into the detergent, wash it with a few towels to help remove the dirt.

Cleaning Your Shower Head and Removing Limescale

- Add 2 cups of vinegar to a bucket
- Fill the bucket with water
- Remove the shower head and place it in the bucket— leave it overnight

Removing Limescale from the Sink

- Scrape the limescale buildup using a butter knife being careful not to scrape too hard or you will damage the porcelain
- Wipe around the sink with a damp cloth
- For really tough stains, add one cup of baking soda and one cup of vinegar to a bowl and stir it together to form a paste
- Lather it around the sink and leave it for an hour
- Rinse the sink and then wipe it with a cloth

How to Clean Bathroom Mirrors

- Fill a spray bottle with warm soapy water
- Wipe the mirror off using paper from a magazine or a sheet of newspaper
- Buff with a dry sheet of paper

How to Clean the Bathtub

- Combine one part white vinegar, one part baking soda, and one part water in a bucket
- Stir to combine
- Soak a sponge in the mixture and scrub the tub with the hard side of the sponge
- Once the entire tub has been cleaned, rinse it with water

HOW TO CLEAN YOUR BEDROOM

Your bed is the most important part of your bedroom. To keep the room and your bedding presentable, change your bedding every week. Not only will this give your bedroom that extra glow, but it will also preserve your bed linen. Pillowcases have the tendency to get dirty really quickly, so you will need to change them twice a week. Wash your comforter once a month.

How to Clean Bedspreads and Blankets

Check the label to see whether you will need to dry clean your bedspreads or blankets. In most cases, you can put them in the washing machine.

Satin or silk bedding is slightly different and will probably need to go to the dry cleaners. Washing them on the wrong temperature or with the wrong detergent will ruin them.

To get rid of stains on your cotton sheets, dip the stain into lemon juice and then put them in the washing machine.

If you have a king-sized bed with large bedding, I suggest taking it to the launderette to get a proper wash. When domestic washing machines are overloaded, they don't do the best of jobs.

How to Clean Blankets

Most people are unaware that blankets collect dust, which is a major contributor to allergies. To get rid of dust, vacuum them every two weeks and then hang them over a clothesline to air. You can then put them in the washing machine.

CHAPTER 8:

DECLUTTERING YOUR RELATIONSHIPS – GETTING RID OF NEGATIVE FRIENDS

There is more to being a minimalist than getting your house and car in order. Messy relationships can weigh you down just as much as a messy house. Negative friends can rob you of your peace of mind, happiness, and your ability to move forward in life and achieve your goals. Have you ever heard the saying "misery loves company?" Well, once your negative friends see that you are trying to change your life for the better, they will do everything in their power to drag you down. Positive and negative don't mix, and unless your friends want to change too, there is no point in staying in the relationship because you will quickly revert back to your old ways. Think about it like this, imagine standing on a table and trying to pull someone up to stand on it with you. It's impossible. They will end up pulling you down, and that's what happens with negative friends when you attempt to walk in a different direction. You desperately want them to come on your journey with you, but they are not ready to make that change so you try to pull them up, but they end up pulling you down. Here are five reasons you need to get rid of negative friends if you want to successfully declutter your life.

1. **Negative Friends Don't Have Your Best Interests at Heart**

   The main aim of a friendship is to empower each other, not drag each other down. Friends are supposed to assist you in getting to the next level in life; therefore, it is important that you associate with people who are of the same mindset as you.

   Negative friends don't really care about you as a person. All they care about is themselves, and they will drain your energy, making sure that their needs are always met at your expense. They don't care about how you might be feeling or what you might be going through when they decide that they want your help; their main concern is that they get what they want.

2. **Negative Friends Drain Your Energy**

   Negative friends always have some drama going on in their lives that they need you to assist them with. They are extremely pessimistic and they always have something negative to say about the positive advice you attempt to give them. Because they are so negative, they attract negative situations in their lives, hence the constant drama that you end up getting caught up in because you're their friend. These people don't lift you up, they bring you down, and when you are around them you feel as though you are being suffocated by a cloud of negative black smoke. These are not the type of people you want in your life. You need to be around people who are going to encourage you to become the best version of yourself and achieve the goals you have set. If you feel depleted any time you are around certain friends, you are going to have to get rid of them.

3. **Negative Friends Don't Want You to Succeed**

Have you ever told a friend about something you hoped to achieve and all they could do was discourage you with statements like, "Are you sure this is a good idea? It sounds really risky," or "There are too many problems, I don't think you will be able to overcome them."

Or they try to guilt-trip you by saying things like, "What about me? I thought we would ride or die forever."

Statements like this are not encouraging you to succeed, they are encouraging you to stay in the predicament you are in so that you will never move forward in life. Negative friends are so selfish. All they care about is themselves, so much so that when it comes to your plans for the future, they think they have the right to be included, and if they are not, then you are the bad guy for abandoning them.

4. **Your Potential for Greatness is at Risk**

As you have just read, negative friends will do everything in their power to prevent you from becoming successful in life. Once they can see that you are actively taking steps to better yourself, they become like crabs in a bucket and try to pull you back down. Such people can rob you of your chance to become great. You see, it's easier to be negative than to be positive. The world is in total chaos; all you have to do is turn on the TV or open a newspaper and all you see is doom and gloom. Negative friends will remind you of everything that's wrong with the world, wrong with you, and wrong with them. All of which is an attempt to get you to give up on your dreams. Their ultimate goal is to convince you that the world is hopeless and so are you, so there is simply no point in trying.

It is essential that you let go of anyone who is opposed to where you want to go in life. Oil and water don't mix, neither do negative and positive—it's either one or the other! It will be impossible for you to become a positive person and live your best life with negative friends. You put yourself in harm's way when you surround yourself with people who are not walking in the same direction as you.

5. **Negative People Will Ruin Your Reputation**

Have you ever heard the saying that birds of a feather flock together? Well, if you hang around with negative Nancy's, people are going to assume you are the same way. When you decide to change your life, it's not that you think you are now better than your friends, you have just come to the realization that if you want to succeed in life then you are going to have to change your attitude. Once you change your attitude, you also need to change your friends to suit your new attitude. One thing you don't want is to ruin your chances of making new positive friends because you won't let go of negative friends. Positive people want to be around positive people.

As you have read this, you have probably come to the realization that there are a few people in your life that you need to get rid of, and this is not an easy task. At the end of the day, there is a possibility that you have been friends with such people since high school, and it's simply not that easy to cut them out of your life. But let me tell you, if you don't, the universe will. Here's an example.

My older sister (we'll call her Jessica) is an artist. She is 42 years old and had been best friends with a girl (we'll call her Sandy) since she was 18; they went to high school together. Sandy is a party girl. She is very self-centered, loves attention, and is always in a bad relationship that revolves around an insane amount of drama. Sandy went out every weekend and dragged my sister along with her; however, when my sister decided that it was time to get serious with her art, the dynamics of their relationship changed. Jessica could no longer spend as much time with Sandy as she used to, and Sandy didn't like it. To cut a long story short, Sandy decided to make other friends so she could continue her party life. One day, Sandy invited Jessica out with her new friends, for old times' sake she decided to go, and it was a complete disaster!

My sister was not the same person and was no longer interested in fruitless gossip and the drama that surrounded Sandra's life. Her new friends were exactly the same as Sandy and didn't like Jessica's positive vibes. Whenever she attempted to change the conversation, they would get irate and accuse my sister of being a killjoy. That night they had a massive argument and haven't spoken since. A twenty plus-year friendship was destroyed in one night because my sister had decided to take a different direction in life. The good news is that since their split, she has become a very successful artist and made new friends that are on the same wavelength as her.

When it comes to eliminating negative people from your life, you don't want to do so on bad terms. Having enemies is never a good idea so here are a few strategies to assist you in getting rid of the negative Nancy's in your life.

Create Boundaries and Maintain Them: There are some people, like family members and work colleagues, that you can't totally eliminate from your life. So, the most effective way of dealing with such people is to create boundaries and maintain them. In other words, feed them with a long-handled spoon. The first thing you need to do is decide what you will tolerate in a relationship and what you won't. By the way, this is not only something you should do with people you currently know now, but also with new people you meet. When you start to feel that something is not right in your interactions with people, enforce your boundaries and don't back down.

For example, if you have a friend who is always calling you to complain about something, tell him or her that you would appreciate when they call you that they either have something good to say or they don't bother calling you at all. Once that friend realizes that you are serious, and they are not willing to change, they will simply stop calling you because they won't have anything to call you about.

Don't Allow Yourself to be Manipulated: Toxic people always have some emergency crisis that they need you to assist them with. They will call you screaming and crying that you need to come around urgently, and when you get there you find out that it's something as miniscule as they've broken a fingernail! We've all heard the story of the boy who cried wolf, but there may be that one time when there really is an emergency. So, before you leave your house, make sure the issue isn't something you can resolve over the phone instead of wasting your time and just dashing over there.

Understand Projection: Eliminating negative people from your life is a process, and a part of that process involves limiting the amount of power they have over your emotions, and that means understanding that when they are hurting you, they are not really seeing you. What they are actually doing is projecting the parts about themselves that they don't like onto you, and this is usually done via a verbal attack. Their vicious behavior has nothing to do with you, but everything to do with how much they hate themselves.

Don't Give Up: When your negative friends realize that you are no longer falling for their games and are trying to distance yourself, their behavior will get a lot worse. It can become so intense that some people fold and give in to their demands. You have to be relentless. Remind yourself that this is for your benefit and theirs; hopefully, you pulling away might force them to take a good look in the mirror and change their behavior. Either way, once they realize that you are no longer willing to tolerate their antics, they will find another victim to attack.

Get Some New Friends: You are probably going to feel pretty lonely once you have gotten rid of your negative friends; not to worry, you can make new ones. Make a conscious effort to go out to different places. If you don't already have one, start a hobby, or take up a sport or a craft. Be friendly, walk around with a smile on your face, and become the type of person you want to attract.

CHAPTER 9:

DECLUTTERING YOUR THOUGHTS – GETTING YOUR MIND OUT OF THE GUTTER

When you go to sleep at night do you nod off peacefully, or do you lay your head on the pillow with a mind full of chaos and confusion? Most people will agree with the latter. Not only are our homes full of clutter, but our minds are also full of clutter; the average brain is in constant overdrive, thinking, worrying, and being anxious about upcoming events. There is actually nothing wrong with thinking as long as your thoughts are positive and helpful; unfortunately, that is not the case for most of us.

The universe is made up of laws, and there is nothing we can do to change them. If we choose to live by them, they will work for us; if not, they will work against us. The reality is that your current life situation, whether good or bad, is due to the way you think. Your reality is created by your state of mind. Think about it like this, before anything manifests in the physical world, it starts as a thought. The lightbulb was invented by Thomas Edison before the bulb became a reality; he sat down and thought about what it would be like to have a light that you could turn off and on instead of lighting a candle. He then thought about how he could make this device, and then he went on to make it. The light bulb and every other creation in the world started with a thought. If you want to organize your life, the first thing you need to take control of is your thought life. As your thinking pattern is transformed from negative to positive, you will begin to experience a healthy shift in your current reality.

Society teaches us that our feelings are defined by our circumstances when the truth is that our feelings are defined by our thoughts. Every area of your life, from your finances to your health and relationships, are a direct result of your thoughts and your overall belief system. Since we cannot change this reality, the only thing we can do is accept it and make the decision to take dominion over our thoughts instead of them having control over us. Only then will you be able to transform your life and attract the things that you want.

There are no constraints on your thought life, no one can dictate to you how you should think; you are in the driver's seat. Nobody else has access to your mind apart from you; in fact, it is the most powerful possession you own, and once you tap into this reality, you will become unstoppable.

Science continues to confirm that everything in the universe, including our thoughts, is made up of energy. This means that your thoughts are alive, and each time you think about something, depending on what you are thinking about, that energy is either positive or negative.

This book is not about the law of attraction; however, I feel that it is important to mention it here to give you a better understanding of how your thoughts are affecting your life. The main premise of the law of attraction is that energy is like a magnet, it attracts other energy. So, if your thoughts are energy, you attract what you think. There is a value attached to each thought; however, this is something that you determine. The more you think about something, the more powerful that thought becomes and the faster you will see it turn into a reality. The random thoughts you think are not as powerful as your consistent thoughts. However, it is important to mention that if you spend one hour a day thinking positive, but 23 hours a day thinking negative, it is your negative thoughts that will hold the most power. Negative thinking overshadows positive thinking, and positive thinking overshadows negative thinking. Therefore, you create your reality according to what you think about the most.

The mind is made up of two compartments, the conscious and the subconscious mind. The majority of people are unaware of the subconscious mind and how powerful it is. You can compare the subconscious mind to a gigantic warehouse that stores every experience you have ever encountered in life. According to experts, by the age of 21, the subconscious mind has already stored the equivalent of the contents of 100 Encyclopedia Britannica's! During hypnosis, older people are capable of remembering with complete accuracy, things that took place in their life 50 years previously. The subconscious mind is in perfect condition, the problem is the conscious mind.

The subconscious mind is designed to store and retrieve information. Its job is to ensure that your behavior is in alignment with the way you have been programmed. Your words and actions fit a pattern shaped out of the self-concept created by your subconscious mind. There is nothing that the subconscious mind does independently; the only thing it does is obey the orders given to it by the conscious mind. Think about it like this, the job of a gardener is to plant seeds in fertile soil; well, your subconscious mind is the fertile soil, it is made up of the perfect conditions for seeds to take root and grow. So, if your mind plays the role of a gardener and plants seeds of thought into your subconscious mind, it means that whether the thoughts are positive or negative, they are going to grow, and it is these thoughts that are the driving force behind your life.

Your subconscious mind doesn't have a voice. It does not have the ability to tell your conscious mind to stop sending it thoughts, so the seeds that are sown will either become beautiful flowers that will guide you to live your best life or ugly weeds that will ensure all your worst nightmares come true. You are the only person who can choose which seeds are planted.

Those who were brought up in an abusive household hold a memory bank of everything that took place during those years. If you have never been able to understand why there are some people who walk out of one abusive relationship right into another—this is why. The only reality that their subconscious mind knows is abuse; therefore, abuse has become their physical reality and that is what they attract. Even though they know that it is wrong for them to be treated the way they are, and they have a deep desire to get as far away from an abusive partner as possible, they are continuously drawn back because that is what they attract. If they don't get professional help, most people give up and end up believing that is what they deserve in life, and oftentimes, they pass it onto their children. The cycle of abuse then continues until someone gets fed up and puts an end to it.

This all sounds really gloomy, doesn't it? No, it's not a position that anyone wants to be in; but the good news is that there is a way out. You can declutter your mind and live the life that you deserve.

CHAPTER 10:

DECLUTTERING YOUR THOUGHTS – THE POWER OF POSITIVE THINKING

To declutter your mind, you will need to learn to change the way you think. This is not an easy task, but neither is it impossible. From my own personal experience, I can tell you that focusing on the positive instead of the negative will bring much good into your life. However, before I dive into that, what do you think happy and successful people spend their time thinking about? This answer is pretty simple really. They think about the goals they have set for themselves and how they intend to accomplish them. These thoughts shield their minds from negative thinking and help them to develop a positive attitude that propels them into success. On the flip side of things, negative people spend their time thinking and talking about what they don't have and what they don't want in life, which makes them feel miserable and depressed.

How to Develop a Positive Mindset

According to research, positive people are very optimistic. Even in difficult times, they are able to change their perspective and see the light at the end of the tunnel. I refer to these people as eagles. You see, an eagle is one of the strongest birds in nature. When a storm is brewing, all the other birds fly off and hide. However, the eagle loves storms; in fact, they wait in anticipation for them. Eagles like to fly high, and the force of a storm allows them to do so. When the storm arrives, they tilt their body in a certain angle and allow the winds to take them higher. This is what positive people do. They see the storms or problems in their lives different from everyone else, and that's because they look at them from a different angle. They see them as opportunities and use them to push them into something greater. This is not the case with negative people; like the other birds, they run and hide from their problems and see them as the end instead of the beginning. Being positive is all about one thing, and that is state of mind.

The good news about optimism is that it is a quality that you can learn. If you say and do what positive people do, you will become like them. Optimists look for the treasure in every dark place. Instead of getting angry and depressed, they get their emotions in check and say, "What lessons can I learn from what has taken place?" They don't have sleepless nights worrying about their situation; they find solutions and get to work so that they can resolve their problems.

How to Train Your Brain to Think Positive

Training the brain is a simple concept; it is putting it into practice and making it a habit that is difficult. Do you remember what you learned about the subconscious mind? Well, when you decide that you are going to do something that your subconscious mind does not recognize, it will do everything it can to pull you back into your old habits. This is the reason why bad habits are so difficult to break—you are literally fighting against yourself and it doesn't feel very good. The subconscious mind wants to keep you in your comfort zone, and if you are used to thinking negative all the time, thinking positive is stepping outside of your comfort zone. The trick is to push through, and if you mess up, keep going. They say it takes 60 days to develop a habit, so keep working at it and you will eventually get there.

Despite the fact that the mind is an incredibly powerful tool, it only has the capacity to focus on one thought at a time; therefore, your goal is to keep on thinking positive thoughts until new neural pathways are created in the brain. Remember, when something negative happens, the way you respond to it will determine the outcome. That's why it is essential to always look for the positive in any negative situation.

THE POWER OF POSITIVE AFFIRMATIONS

Affirmations are either the words that you say or the thoughts that you think. If you are reading this, there is a high chance you have a habit of saying and thinking not very nice things, which means that your mind is basically full of junk. Positive affirmations open the door to transformation. Let me ask you a question: who is the person you speak to the most? Most people are going to say their boyfriend, girlfriend, or best friend. The truth is that the person you speak to the majority of the time is yourself. We all have an internal dialog, and we are either saying nice things to ourselves or not very nice things. There are several health benefits associated with positive affirmations:

It Eliminates Depression: There are several reasons people suffer from depression; but some of them are low self-esteem, not feeling worthy, and not feeling good enough. Research has found that repeating positive affirmations can help to reverse depression. A study conducted by the University of Arizona found that positive affirmations were an effective supplemental treatment for patients suffering from depression and anxiety. For some of the patients, positive affirmations were more helpful than drugs or therapy.

How to Use Positive Affirmations

There are three ways that you can use positive affirmations. For them to be the most effective, I would strongly advise that you use all three.

1. **Thought Replacement:** The majority of the time we don't even realize what we are thinking about. According to experts, we think between 12,000-70,000 thoughts per day! That's a lot of thoughts; however, these are automatic thoughts that we will never remember. If I told you to write down your last 1,000 thoughts, you would look at me like I was crazy. These are not the thoughts you need to be concerned about, because they are not the thoughts you focus on. The trick is that you need to catch yourself when you are thinking negative thoughts and replace them with a positive affirmation.

2. **Affirmation Repetition:** This involves setting aside a time each day and standing in front of a mirror and repeating affirmations.

3. **Affirmation Meditation:** No, I am not talking about the type of meditation that involves sitting with your legs crossed and chanting. You can also meditate by repeating words continuously. This is also referred to as murmuring. The aim of affirmation meditation is to get you into the habit of thinking positive so that there is no room in your mind to think negative thoughts. The aim is to spend the entire day silently saying affirmations under your breath. If there is no one around, you can say them out loud.

HERE ARE 25 POSITIVE AFFIRMATIONS TO GET YOU OUT OF THE HABIT OF NEGATIVE THINKING.

1. I will live the life of my dreams.
2. I possess the tools I need to succeed in life.
3. I am stronger than my struggles.
4. I am in control of my life.
5. I am fierce.
6. I have the power to motivate myself.
7. I will achieve every goal I have set for myself.
8. I am not afraid of the fire because I am the fire.
9. I deserve the best out of life and nothing less.
10. I have the choice to decide who I become in life.
11. I am allowed to say "no" sometimes.
12. Happiness is a reality for me.
13. I speak with self-assurance and confidence.
14. There are no limits to my confidence.
15. I am worthy to be loved unconditionally.
16. I choose to be hopeful instead of fearful.
17. I choose to be positive instead of negative.

18. I will not allow other people's negative emotions to affect me.

19. I am committed to becoming the best version of myself.

20. I am not defined by my circumstances.

21. I am bold and beautiful.

22. I love myself unconditionally.

23. I am responsible for creating the life that I want.

24. I will only think thoughts of peace, love, and harmony.

25. I will not waste my energy on negative self-talk.

CHAPTER 11:

DECLUTTERING YOUR DAY –
ENHANCING YOUR TIME
MANAGEMENT SKILLS

D o you feel as if there are not enough hours in the day to get things done? If you answered yes to this question, it's probably because you spend too much time doing fruitless activities that you don't get time to do what really needs to be done. According to statistics, the average American household spends 7 hours and 50 minutes watching TV per day. So, people are not spending their time doing constructive and beneficial activities that will enhance their lives, like reading, studying or exercising; they are slumped in front of a TV! To compound the issue, we are now living in an era where social media has taken over the world. Research suggests that the average person spends around two hours per day on social media! So, if there are only 24 hours in a day and eight of those are spent asleep, that means we are awake for 16 hours per day. And fourteen of them per week are spent with our eyes glued to a screen! Not to mention all the other things we are doing in between. Can you see why you never get anything done?

One of the main differences between the successful and the unsuccessful people in the world is that they know how to manage their time, and they are extremely particular about it. Let's take a look at some of their daily routines.

Sir Richard Branson is the founder of the Virgin Group conglomerate, and he has a net worth of $5 billion. In a 2014 blog post, Branson documented his daily routine, which included:

- Waking up at 5:00 am
- Breakfast with his family
- Responding to emails
- Yoga and Tai Chi
- Carrying a notebook to write down inspiration throughout the day
- Rarely watches TV
- Dinner with family
- In bed by 11:00 pm

Bill Gates is the founder of Microsoft and is known as one of the wealthiest men in the world. According to Forbes, he has an estimated net worth of $96.5 billion.

- Wakes up at 4:30 am
- Works out on the treadmill at the same time as watching teaching DVDs
- Reads the newspaper
- He breaks up his schedule into five-minute intervals
- He keeps track of his exceptionally busy day by note taking
- Spends time reading

- When he is not working, he enjoys spending time with his three children
- He enjoys playing bridge on the weekends
- He washes the dishes every night

Elon Musk is the CEO and founder of Neuralink and Tesla; he has a net worth of $19.8 billion.

- Wakes up at 7:00 AM
- Checks and responds to emails
- Interacts with his sons and sends them to school
- Takes a shower and makes his way to work
- He refuses to waste time on anything that doesn't make things better
- In his free time, he enjoys hanging out with friends, watching movies, and playing games with his children

Warren Buffet is the most successful investor in the world; he has an estimated net worth of $77.7 billion.

- He wakes up at 6:45 AM
- Reads *Forbes, USA Today*, and the *Wall Street Journal*
- Has breakfast
- Does some exercise
- Goes to work and spends 80% of his day reading
- Unwinds after work by playing bridge
- Goes to bed at 10:45 PM

Okay, so we have looked at the daily routines of some of the most successful people in the world, and one thing they have in common is that they all use their time very productively. Did you notice that there was no mention of watching TV? These people are billionaires and run multibillion-dollar corporations, yet they still find time for leisure activities and spending time with their families.

If you want to get more done during the day and achieve the goals that you have set for yourself, you are going to need to completely rearrange your life and do some careful planning. Most people will admit that their daily routine looks something like this:

- Set the alarm for 7:00 am but hit the snooze button until 7:30 am
- Jump out of bed and take a shower
- Get the kids ready (if you have them)
- Rush out the door
- Grab breakfast on the go
- Work for 8 hours
- Come home
- Have dinner
- Sit in front of the TV
- Go to bed
- Repeat until the weekend

Here are a few tips to assist you in managing your time better so that you can be more productive throughout the day.

Create a Daily Routine: We all know how important it is for children to have a daily routine to give them some discipline and structure. I am sure you can remember being told what time to go to bed, wake up, have dinner, do your homework, etc. when you were younger. But as you grew older, this routine became less and less important until you collapsed into a very unorganized life schedule with no boundaries. I am sure you can admit this. The majority of adults don't have a set routine and just go through their day without a plan and hope for the best. The way a child feels stressed and anxious when they have no routine is the same way adults feel stressed and anxious when they have no routine, but they just don't realize that something so simple is the main cause of their frustration in life.

Many people share the view that routines are boring, stifling, and rigid; but as you have learned from the lives of highly successful people, a strict daily routine is actually the path to productivity, freedom, happiness, and becoming the best version of ourselves. Here are a few benefits associated with having a daily routine.

Creates Structure: A daily routine gives us the much-needed structure and logical sequence required to live our lives and go about our daily affairs. After some time, this routine becomes a habit and we become comfortable and familiar with what we have to do each day.

Establishes Good Habits: Repetition is the secret to building good habits. When we create a personal routine, it helps us develop good habits as we repeat the same tasks each day. Think about it like this: at a minimum, the majority of people brush their teeth first thing in the morning—it's automatic, you don't even think about it, you just do it. Once your daily routine becomes a habit, it too will become automatic.

Break Bad Habits: A daily routine will not only help you build good habits, but it will also help you break bad habits because your good habits will slowly start to replace the bad ones.

Get Our Priorities in Order: There are certain things in your life that are more important than others; however, much of the time they don't get done because other non-essential activities take their place. When you have a routine in place, you know exactly what you need to do on any given day.

Eliminates Procrastination: When routine becomes habit, as mentioned, we just do things automatically. So we are basically doing things subconsciously, which eliminates procrastination and enables us to quickly do the things we need to do without continuously putting them off to the following day.

Builds Momentum: Momentum is very important when it comes to achieving goals. When you think about the end result, getting there seems impossible; however, if you are doing something small each day to get to your final destination, you are more likely to get there.

Builds Self Confidence: When you are unable to achieve your goals or you are constantly leaving projects undone, it is soul destroying. There is no one to blame other than yourself, and this is not something you want to make a habit out of. However, when you have a strict routine in place and you are constantly working towards your goals, confidence is built as you achieve them.

Wake Up Early: We have all heard the saying, "The early bird gets the worm," and as you read, all of the successful people mentioned waking up before 7:00 AM. There are several benefits to waking up early.

- **Time to Yourself:** This is especially true if you have children. In the early hours of the morning when no one is awake, there are no cars outside, no noise, just you and your thoughts. It's a good time to think and reflect and decide how you are best going to tackle your day. It allows you to prepare yourself to start your routine instead of jumping out of bed and springing into action because you don't have the time.

- **Increased Productivity:** Since everyone else is asleep, waking up early allows you to get things done while there are no distractions. For example, if one of your goals is to write a book, you can use this time to write a few pages. Writing a book is a huge task; however, a journey of a thousand miles starts with a single step. Even if you write one page a day, you can write a book within a year.

- **Makes You Feel More Positive:** A sense of achievement is a great feeling, and you are more likely to experience this when you wake up early. You see, extra time means that you can get more things done, like having breakfast, exercising, or working on a project. You will no longer feel the same pressure and stress of when you wake up late and have to rush around trying to get things done.

- **Peak Will Power:** Studies have shown that will power is at its peak first thing in the morning. The best time to work on your goals is after you've had a good night's sleep and your energy has been renewed. As you go throughout the day, your energy and will power is depleted, and so when you return home after a hard day's work you are less likely to do the things you had planned.

- **Peaceful Commute:** Whether you drive to work or get public transport everyone can relate to the stress of rush hour traffic. The good news is that when you wake up early and leave the house early, you avoid this. It allows you to get to work before everyone else and get ahead of your deadlines.

TO-DO LISTS

Do you constantly feel overwhelmed because of all the things that you need to get done? Do you forget to do certain things? Or miss deadlines? If you have answered yes to any of these questions, then a to-do list will help you organize and prioritize your tasks.

By writing a list of things that you need to do, you ensure that everything you need to accomplish is written down in front of you so that you don't leave anything out. And by listing the activities in order of importance, you can prioritize which of them you are going to do first. To-do lists are crucial if you are going to overcome work overload. However, there is more to it than simply writing out a list, you must learn to use them effectively. Here are some tips to help you.

Step 1: Make a list of all the tasks you need to get out of the way. If you have a lot of different things to get done, you might find it easier to write several lists, for example, work, study, home.

Step 2: Put a letter or a number next to each task to list them in order of priority and then write the list out again in order.

Step 3: Work your way through the list in order and as you complete each task, tick them off the list.

To-do List Software: Using paper is a great way to get started writing to-do lists but you can be much more efficient using software. You will need to take some time out to teach yourself how to use the software, but once you've mastered it, you'll find the program very easy to use. One of the main benefits of using software is that it reminds you of things you need to get done urgently, and you can synchronize it with your email and phone so that you always have your list at hand. A Google search will pull up a list of recommended software.

Goal Setting: When was the last time you set a goal for yourself and actually achieved it? The sad truth is that the average person doesn't set goals, they simply coast through life, and then when they reach 50 wonder why they haven't achieved anything significant. As you have probably realized by now, time waits for no man, and so the most essential element of time is what you choose to do with it. Therefore, setting goals for yourself and timeframes in which to accomplish them is one of the most productive things you can do.

When deciding what to do with your time, your main focus should be on your goals and how everything you do is aimed at bringing you a little bit closer to achieving those goals.

WHY SET GOALS?

Entrepreneurs, athletes, and high achievers in any career all set goals for themselves. Goal setting provides you with something to focus on for the long term and motivation to achieve for the short term. They allow you to use the knowledge that you have already gained to assist you in making the most out of your life. By setting goals that are concise and clear, you can keep track of your progress and feel good about yourself once you have achieved them. When you get the dream out of your head and put it down on paper, it turns a seemingly impossible task into something realistic.

WHERE DO I START?

Now that you have decided on what goals you want to achieve, it is important that you make a plan to achieve them. Think about it this way, if you are about to drive to a destination you are not familiar with, do you use a GPS to get you to your location or waste time driving around all over town trying to find it? Well, the same principle applies in life—you can either drift around aimlessly without any direction or focus, or you can make a plan.

Goal setting is a powerful process that allows you to think about the best future for yourself, which then provides the motivation to push you towards achieving your goals. Goal setting helps you decide what direction you want to take in life. When you know where you want to go, you know where to keep your focus, and you stop wasting time on fruitless activities that distract you from doing what needs to be done to accomplish your goals.

When it comes to writing down your goals don't be shy, there is nothing wrong with dreaming big. After all, where would we be in the world today if people didn't dream big? Things like the laptop I am using to type this book would never have been invented. So, that gigantic mansion you can see yourself living in, write it down. The word "dream" is often misused; the assumption is that because something can't be seen with the natural eye it can't be a reality. For example, if you tell someone that you have a dream of owning your own business one day when you are working in a factory on minimum wage, that person will most likely look at you as if you have lost your mind because you don't have the required credentials. Your dream is specific to you; it belongs to you, and you have the ability to turn it into a reality—don't let anyone tell you otherwise.

When you write your end goal down on paper, it is going to look intimidating. Your first thought is going to be, "Well, how am I ever going to achieve something like this?" Not to worry, there is a strategy, and if you follow it, success is inevitable.

When you set lifetime goals, it clarifies your perspective and becomes the driving force behind the decisions that you make. If you are not sure about the goals you should be setting for yourself, here are a few ideas.

Career: What level do you want to get to in your career? Do you want to become a partner, a CEO, a manager?

Financial: How much money do you want to earn? If you are in a career that won't give you this opportunity, you will need to switch careers.

Education: To achieve your career goals, are there certain qualifications you will need to acquire? For example, if you want to become an accountant, what certifications would you need to get?

Family: Do you have a desire to get married by a certain age? Would you like to have children? If so, how many? Do you have an ideal partner in mind?

Attitude: Are there things about your character that you would like to change? Do you get angry easily? Are you easily offended?

Physical: Do you consider yourself to be overweight? Do you have an ideal body type that you would wish to achieve?

Public Service: Are there things you would like to do in the community? Are there people you would like to help?

Spend some time brainstorming some ideas. There is no need to go overboard, you don't want to choose goals in every category and overwhelm yourself. It is advised that you have no more than 10 significant goals.

GOAL BREAKDOWN

Once you have determined what your lifetime goals are, write out a five-year plan that details the smaller goals you will need to accomplish to achieve the larger ones.

Your next step should be to write out a list of daily goals you will need to achieve to turn your ultimate goal into a reality. For example, if you need to gain qualifications for career goals, your short-term goals should be a daily study plan to ensure you have the knowledge to pass your exams. The idea is to take micro steps towards your goals instead of trying to rush them when you realize the deadline is fast approaching.

STAY ON TRACK

Don't work blindly—pay attention to what you are doing at all times. A good way to do this is to set yourself weekly reminders to check how far you have progressed. If you are not where you need to be, you will need to figure out why and come up with another strategy.

S.M.A.R.T Goals

A great way to get the most out of the goal-setting process is to use the SMART technique. SMART stands for: Specific, Measurable, Attainable, Relevant and Timely. There are several versions of this type of goal setting, but in general, the SMART method helps you get more specific about your goals. For example, you wouldn't just write, "I want to become a lawyer." You would write, "I want to become a lawyer by December 2020." The idea is that once you put a date on a goal, it prevents you from procrastinating and encourages you to take steps towards the goal.

Bonus Goal Setting Tips

Turn your goals into a positive affirmation: Instead of writing, "I want to get married and have three children by the age of 35." Write, "I am married with three children by the age of 35." When you speak about a goal in the present tense, the subconscious mind records the information as if it has already taken place. This process makes manifestation easier.

Be Specific: If you are not sure about what you want, achieving it is going to be difficult. Make sure that you are extremely specific about what you want down to very last detail. Include information such as dates, times, and amounts.

Set Priorities: Some of your goals are going to be more important to you than others; therefore, list your goals in order of priority and work on them in that order.

Be Realistic: I encourage everyone I know to dream big; however, it is also important that you are realistic, or you will set yourself up for failure. For example, having a goal that you will lose 20 lbs. in one week is not a good idea.

Don't stop once you have achieved your goals—life should never become stagnant. Always have something to focus on, that motivates you, and pushes you forward. In fact, one of your most important goals should be continuous self-improvement.

STOP PROCRASTINATING

One of the most dangerous dream killers is procrastination—time waits for no man, and it isn't going to wait for you. Procrastination is delaying things that you could do today until the following day. Before you know it, ten years have passed without you achieving your goal!

Procrastination is often taken as a joke, or spoken of lightly, when in reality it is an extremely destructive force that has the power to stop you from moving forward in life. If procrastination is something you want to eradicate from your life, this chapter will help you to do so.

1. **Recognizing Procrastination:** The majority of people know full well when they are procrastinating. It's not difficult to work out that you have a deadline in an hour, but you are emailing your boyfriend about your upcoming romantic getaway! Here are some of the main symptoms of procrastination.

   • You have several things to do within the day but none of them are important

   • Getting ready to complete something and then deciding that you need a cup of coffee or a sandwich

- Leaving the most important jobs on your to-do list until last

- Waiting until you feel like doing something before getting on with it

It's also important to mention what procrastination isn't—leaving insignificant tasks until a later date. There will be times when there are some things that have to be put on hold because something else is more important. For example, you may have a deadline, but you also have a doctor's appointment that you have to attend. There are also going to be times when you simply don't have the energy to do certain tasks. If you are tired, sleep—it's important that you listen to your body so you don't end up doing a bad job, or worse, get sick from overworking yourself.

WHY DO YOU PROCRASTINATE?

There are many different reasons people procrastinate. If the task is something that you don't enjoy doing, you are going to put it off for as long as you can. All jobs are going to have things about them that we don't like. The key is to get them done so that we can put our energy into the aspects of the job that we like.

In general, disorganized people don't have a specific system in place when it comes to doing certain things. So they just do things with their eyes closed and hope for the best. Organized people, on the other hand, create to-do lists and schedules that have been prioritized. They take note of when the task must be completed, the importance attached to each task, and the length of time it will take to complete the task. Organized people are also good at just getting things done. They stay away from procrastination and they don't like being unproductive. They make life easier for themselves by breaking each activity down into manageable chunks so that the project doesn't overwhelm them.

Some people are intimidated by certain tasks because they know that they don't have the skills required to get it done, and therefore, focus on things that they know they can complete so they don't have to deal with feeling inadequate. Then there are some people who are afraid of success—they don't like failure either—but success scares them even more. Any amount of success is going to be life changing because it brings on additional responsibility, and there are some people who don't want to deal with that.

STRATEGIES TO PREVENT PROCRASTINATION

Procrastination is a habit—it isn't something that you developed overnight, so don't expect it to disappear overnight. You are going to have to put some work in if you want to overcome it. A habit is no longer a habit once you have stopped participating in it. You are more likely to eradicate procrastination from your life if you implement as many of these strategies as possible. Go through each one and decide what works best for you.

Consequences: Focus your mind on what will happen if you miss the deadline. Is there a possibility that you might get a disciplinary warning? Could you lose pay? If you are self-employed will it mean a bad review?

Reward Yourself: Rewarding yourself is a great incentive to get things done. It doesn't need to be anything big, whether it's a new pair of shoes, a movie, or a bar of chocolate, establish a system of reward that's going to motivate you to get things completed.

Accountability Partner: Having someone to report to is a bit like peer pressure. Most people don't want to look like a fool in front of their friends, so they will do what needs to be done to impress them. Diet clubs and self-help groups swear by this method because it works so well.

Get Organized: This is a no brainer really, but it's worth mentioning to remind you of how important it really is. Organization is the key to success. Here are a few tips you can implement to become more organized and avoid procrastination.

1. **Plan Your Projects:** Create a schedule for each day that details the process you are going to take for completing each task and how long it will take for you to get them done.

2. **To do Lists:** This is another reminder, but it's important—to do lists help you to stay on top of things. When you attempt to remember what you need to do, you are bound to forget.

3. **Set Goals:** In general, you will know how long it is going to take to complete each task. A great way to motivate yourself is to set time goals to finish each task within a certain amount of time.

4. **Don't Multitask:** No matter how many deadlines you've got, never try to do all of them at once. Focus on one task at a time.

So now you know all about procrastination and how to avoid it, that's great. Knowledge is power, but implementation is even more powerful!

CONCLUSION

I have no idea what it is that you want out of life, but what I do know is that you picked up this book because you want things in your life to change. May I submit to you that before you become a public success, you must first become a success in private. What you do behind closed doors is more important than what you do in front of a crowd because what you do in secret is what truly defines your character. Private preparation is how you get ready to go to the next level in your life.

When I started my personal journey to decluttering my life, I had no idea that it would lead me to what I am doing today. Cleaning up and cleaning out placed my feet on the road to success. When my environment was transformed, my mindset was transformed. As my home was renovated, my heart was renovated. Orderliness in my home brought orderliness to my life and that is what propelled me into my purpose in life.

Decluttering my home and getting organized had more to do with getting prepared for my destiny than my house looking like a show home. It's one thing to take the time out to reconstruct your home, but maintenance is an entirely different level of discipline. There are some people who spend every January getting their house in order, but by the end of February, it's a mess again. There is nothing easy about this task by any means. In fact, it's extremely difficult, and there are going to be days when you simply can't be bothered. However, if you don't want to be average, you can't live like the average person. And this relates to every area of your life, not just your home.

It's up to you to put the demands on your life to improve and grow. Seek after excellence and success will seek after you.

I wish you all the best in your pursuit of living a minimal, decluttered, and organized life!

THANKS FOR READING!

I really hope you enjoyed this book, and most of all got more value from it than you had to give.

It would mean a lot to me if you left an Amazon review – I will reply to all questions asked!

Simply find this book on Amazon, scroll to the reviews section, and click "Write a customer review".

Or please visit www.pristinepublish.com/hyggebundlereview to leave a review

Be sure to check out my email list, where I am constantly adding tons of value. The best way to get on the list currently is by visiting www.pristinepublish.com and entering your email.

Here I'll provide actionable information that aims to improve your enjoyment of life. I'll update you on my latest books, and I'll even send free e-books that I think you'll find useful.

Kindest regards,

Olivia Telford

ALSO BY
Olivia Telford

With Mindfulness you'll discover the secrets of truly calm, contented people. It will guide you to a place of living with more inner peace and fulfillment.

Visit: www.pristinepublish.com/olivia

Manufactured by Amazon.ca
Bolton, ON

23407623R00143